Quantum

Computers

A Complete Guide to Explain in Easy Way

(Mathematical Principle and Transition to the Classical Discrete)

Carlos Price

Published By **Jordan Levy**

Carlos Price

Quantum Computers: A Complete Guide to Explain in Easy Way(Mathematical Principle and Transition to the Classical Discrete)

ISBN   978-1-990373-72-5

Legal & Disclaimer

Table of Contents

Chapter 1: What is Quantum Computing?

Classical computers, the sophisticated that we use every day make use of memory composed of bits. Bits communicate to one or zero; or on or off. Every computer action such as fumbling around, to sending emails, is a result of controlling those and zeros.

Quantum PCs are a different type of PC that utilizes the peculiar properties of quantum materials science in order to resolve problems that are impossible for conventional computers. This is done by using qubits instead of bits. Similar to bits, qubits talk to either an either zero or one. What makes them special is that a qubit could have a single, zero or a combination of both. This means qubits can be zero and one at the same time, which makes quantum computers more dominant than their normal counterparts.

With the help of Superposition technology, quantum computer are able to solve problems that were impossible or take a significant amount of time to complete. Quantum computers far surpass old-fashioned computers, and include huge quantities of similar solutions.

Due to their capability of analysing mixtures and analyzing complex mixtures, quantum computers are likely to be used to break codes and streamlining complicated frameworks. Researchers also anticipate quantum computers to be able to accurately demonstrate events at the subatomic scale, which will be a valuable advantage to science, technology, and research in material science.

Superposition is awe-inspiring yet elusive, fragile, and secretive. The primary obstacle for building fully functional quantum computer is the fact that qubits need to be in a super-cool, disconnected state, or they will decohere in their quantum state and loose the "enchantment."

Quantum computers are on the brink of what is considered common understanding.

Engineers have successfully developed quantum computers, however, until now, they haven't successful in getting enough qubits to work simultaneously to comprehend their full potential but the promise of quantum computing's potential has researchers all over the world working in the direction of making quantum computing among the most significant technological advances of the 21st century.

Imagine a computer with memory that is exponentially greater than its physical size or a computer that could manage an enormous array of information sources simultaneously; one that is able to register in the twilight area that is the size of the room. It's like thinking of the quantum computer. In general, only a handful of fundamental concepts from quantum mechanics can create quantum computers that are feasible. The challenge is the process of determining how to manage these concepts. Are computers like this certain, or would it be difficult to think about creating?

Due to the bizarre quantum mechanics laws, Folger the senior editorial manager at Discover observed that one electron, proton or any other subatomic molecule can be "in more than each spot in turn," because single particles behave as waves. The better locations are various states in which even a tiny bit can be found every moment.

What's the big deal with quantum computing? Imagine you're working in a huge office and you had to retrieve a portfolio that was left in a workspace that was scattered across many workplaces. In the same way, you'd have to walk through the building, opening doors each time in order to locate the folder case. A normal computer has to move through long string of 1's and 0's until it comes to the correct answer. In any case you can imagine a scenario in which, as instead of looking at the same place without anyone other than yourself, you could create the exact many duplicates. As there are rooms in the structure . Each of them could examine each of the offices, and the one who finds the folder case is the real you, making the others disappear. - (David Freeman, discover)

David Deutsch, a physicist at Oxford University, contended that it is possible to build a groundbreaking computer that is based on this reality. in 1994 Peter Shor, a mathematician from AT&T Bell Laboratories in New Jersey and demonstrated that in principle it is possible that an out-and-out quantum computer could calculate the most complex numbers in just a minute or two, an achievement impossible for even the most speedy normal computer. A series of speculations and discussions about the likelihood of developing quantum computers is currently consuming it, but does not completely eliminate the quantum field of research and innovation.

The underlying principles can be traced through to 1981, in which Richard Feynman noticed that physicists often run into difficulties with computation when trying to build a framework where quantum mechanics could occur. The computations, such as the conductivity of electrons, molecules or photons, take an immense amount of time for modern computers. In 1985, in Oxford England, the first description of how quantum computers might perform was presented by David Deutsch's theories. The quantum computer will not only offer the possibility of outperforming the current computers in terms of speed, but it could also perform certain legitimate tasks to which conventional computers were unable to handle.

The research began to investigate the development of an instrument, and after the approval of the public and additional subsidizing by AT&T Bell Laboratories in Murray Hill, New Jersey, an additional member of the group was also included. Subside Shor discovered that quantum computing could dramatically accelerate the process of considering whole numbers. This isn't just an element in small-scale technological advancement, and can help to translate bits of knowledge to be used in certifyable applications, such as like cryptography, for instance.

"There is an expectation toward the finish of the passage that quantum computers may one day become a reality," claims Gilles Brassard of the University of Montreal. Quantum Mechanics give a sudden clarity in the description of the movement of electrons, particles, and photons at the smallest scales. While this data isn't part of the normal family unit usage, it can absolutely apply to every association of subject that we discern, the true benefits of this data are just beginning to become apparent.

In computer systems circuit sheets are created to ensure that either one or zero is spoken to with varying levels of power. The results of one theory does not have any impact on the other. However there is a problem when quantum theories are proposed in the form of an isolated piece of hardware that is present in two distinct substances and they cover each other, affecting both effects on the double. The issues could possibly be resolved with the top quality from the computer of the future, but it's possible to programme the results in that in this way that the negative impacts balance their positive counterparts, while the negative ones reinforce each other.

This quantum framework has the capability to program the conditions into it, validate the right calculation, and then concentrate on the results. Some possible structures have been looked at by scientists who have proposed using molecules, electrons, or particles that are caught in attractive fields. Converging lasers are then used to boost the particles at the right wavelength and then to restore the particles to their original state. A series of heartbeats could be used to demonstrate particles in a manner suitable for our particular conditions.

Another possible explanation offered is suggested by Seth Lloyd of MIT proposed the use of organic metallic polymers (one-dimensional particles that are made from repeating Iotas). The vitality levels of a given molecule will depend on its connections with the iotas that are adjacent to it in the chain. Laser heartbeats could be used to signal flags to the polymer chain. The two closures will create two distinct vitality states.

Another idea was to substitute natural atoms with gems in which information would be stored in the precious stones at specific frequencies which could be made with additional heartbeats. The nuclear cores that rotate in two modes (clockwise either counterclockwise or clockwise) can be altered with the tip of an optical magnifying lens for nuclear that is either "perusing" it's surface or altering it, which clearly could be "expressing" some portion of the data stored. "Monotonous movements of the tip, you could, in the long run, work out any ideal rationale circuit, " DiVincenzo stated.

This force has some serious risks, be that as it is, that these states will need to be isolated from all things including the wandering photon. Outside impacts could gather and create a stray framework track, and it might be able to pivot, and end backwards and causing frequent mistakes. To avoid this from framing new ideas have emerged to address this issue.

Another option involves keeping the calculation short in order to minimize the chance of error; another option is to create repeated duplicates of the data on machines that are discrete and follow the usual (method) to determine the correct responses.

It would, without doubt, allow your preferences and preferences to quantum computers. Therefore, AT&T Bell Laboratories have created an error amendment technique that allows the quantum bit of data will be encoded into each of the nine quantum bits. In the event that one of the nine quantum bits were lost, it would at the time, be possible to recover the information from the data was transmitted. This is the guaranteed location that quantum states will be in before it is transmitted. Furthermore, the iotas' conditions are found in two nations, it is possible that one ended up being contaminated. The quality of the molecule's health could be determined by observing the side of the particle as each side has a distinct reverse extreme.

The entryways that carry the information are generally being studied by scientists in the present, this one quantum rationale door as well as its arrangement of sections to carry out a specific task. One entryway might control the shift from a one to a 0 and then back while another one could use two bits to make the output zero if both are equivalent, but only one is.

The entryways could be a series of particles encased in a beautiful snare, or single molecules that pass across microwave channels. One door might be constructed within the next one or two years, but any computer that is legitimate must have several entry points for a person to be able to live. Tycho Sleator from NYU along with Harald Weinfurter of UIA take an examination of the quantum rationale entrances as simple steps towards constructing the quantum rationale arrangement.

They would still be entranceways with columns that are collaborating. Lasers that shine on particles trigger a progression that begins at one quantum state, and then on to the next. This can modify the kind of collective movement that is possible in the display. Hence an exact frequency of light can be used to regulate the relationships between particles. A term used to describe the clusters is "quantum-dab exhibits" in that each electron is locked to the quantum-dab structure which encode data to carry out scientific tasks ranging from simple expansion to the calculation of these numbers in their entirety.

These "quantum-speck" structures would be constructed using propels, being in the form of tiny semiconductor boxes, with dividers that restrict electrons to the small area of the material. Another way to regulate how data is created. Craig Lent, the primary research scientist behind the project has based this on a model that comprises five quantum dots, one inside and four in the areas in the deals, electrons will be scattered between the two locations.

The hanging of these units would form the rationale circuits that a quantum computer of the future would need. The distance is sufficient for the creation of "paired wires" made of columns of these units, which would flip the state towards the other side, resulting in an inverse chain reaction every one of the states across the wire, similar to like dominoes that transmit latency. A hypothesis about the impact of this kind of technology has been debated and imagined for a long period of time.

In the debates on this issue, the argument that it's possible damage to its capacity is that the computing speed could be able to derail any security efforts specifically the currently Information encryption standard of the NSA. This is useless as the computation would pose an issue for the machine. The final point is that this false reality first showed in the series Quantum Leap, where this breakthrough becomes quickly apparent. When Ziggy the parallel half breed computer that he designed and modified is discussed, the capabilities of a quantum computer mirror the abilities from the computer that is used to create the series' crossover.

What Are Quantum Computing and Quantum Computers?

A large portion of information that we have on consumer gadgets and the most cutting-edge technological advancements is based on the human's growing knowledge of Quantum Mechanics. This relatively new development in material science focuses on the subatomic realm, of the particles and circles that scientists whose names are Greek or Latin letters as well as the research field's plans to manage to predict and control universes that humans cannot be able to observe, but which are already in existence. This is in opposition to the idea of hypothetical research in material science. Avoid (or in the event that you do, place yourself in a secure spot) the flow and ebb Holy Grail of science, the general bound together hypothesis, or the string hypothesis, based on the idea that the befuddling, squawking, and even playing dice Quantum Mechanics gives scientists the study and application to the advancement of data science, computer science and a variety of other fields of design. In any case, it is a proven application that is not like that of the String Hypothesis. In addition even the current advertising of contact screen devices includes the subatomic universe.

A few clarifications of Quantum mechanics to begin. Within the Quantum world it is all bedlam. There is no thing that is able to be predicted at the subatomic realm, as opposed with the world of physical. They can, of course, be managed and controlled to allow for real use. One example of an innovative application for the player shakers Quantum mechanics can be that of the Quantum computer/computing. These aren't typical for conventional transistor-based computers.

With the use of a Quantum Computer, application of subatomic particles as well as their enigmas, like superposition and snare are possible, making the game of dice unsurprising and easily controlled. Scientists will be able perform tasks using quantum information. the main idea here is that properties of quantum systems are able to communicate with information and can be manipulated. The idea was first proposed by the physicist Alan Turing in 1936 and proposed the quantum computer that is widely used today which is also known as"the quantum Turing machine. It is not wrong to declare that rather than the usual bits and bytes. Quantum computers make use of particles from all of the Greek and Latin alphabet set.

In any event, close to one century from now, the quantum computers are still in its infant stage. But, it is no longer being just a topic of research and speculation and is beginning to come to realization in the form of tests and applications. Calculations for such tests are based on the amount that are quantum bits (qubits for short). In addition, research and government offices are currently promoting the development of Quantum computers because of the potential to provide more precise, accurate and faster calculations and counts. Armed personnel will certainly appreciate its ideas.

The majority of the time generally speaking, the Quantum computer is a fantastic computer. Its memory is substantially larger, for example that it is able to provide a bytes (scientists probably don't have yet a name for it) but with a small size like a card or microchip. It can process a large quantity of data sources at once and be significantly faster and more efficient. It is certain to impact our daily life, in the event that

Quantum computers become available in mass production soon. It's also not more accurate to say that Quantum computing could be the destiny of all computers today. In any event it will be revealed in the near future if this advanced technology is too difficult to imagine making.

What is the reason these quantum effects matter?

More than anything it's that they're fascinating. Better yet, they'll prove invaluable to the development of technology in computing and correspondence.

Due to the power of superposition and entrapment Quantum computers are able to handle a variety of estimations simultaneously. Think about this in the following way that a conventional computer is based on ones and zeros Quantum computers be able to utilize zeros, ones, in "superpositions" of ones and zeros. Some difficult tasks that have been for a while considered impossible (or "recalcitrant") for classical computers can be achieved quickly and efficiently with a quantum computer.

What can a quantum computer accomplish that a conventional computer cannot?

Calculating large numbers is the first step. Achieving two huge numbers is not difficult for all computers. But that figuring out the components of an extremely large (state 500-digit) number, however it is considered to be a challenge for any computer of the past. In 1994, mathematician at the Massachusetts Institute of Technology (MIT) Peter Shor, who was employed by AT&T in the year 1994, revealed that if a functioning quantum computer were available and able to process huge numbers with ease.

In any event I'd rather not to take into account huge amounts...

There is no need to calculate huge numbers! This is due to the fact that it's difficult - regardless even for the most powerful computers available in the present. In actual fact, the challenge of computing huge numbers is the reason behind some of our current cryptography. It's based on math-related issues that are difficult to even contemplate solving. RSA encryption, which is the method employed for encoding your Visa number when shopping online, relies completely on the math problem. The website you purchase from will provide you with an immense "open" key (which anybody is able to access) for encoding your credit card details.

The key is actually made up of two huge prime numbers that are which are only known to the seller. The primary way for anyone to get your information is to be aware of the prime numbers which grow to form the key. Because figuring is extremely difficult it is unlikely that a meddler has the ability to access your Visa number, and your ledger will be protected. However, if, for example the case, somebody has created quantum computers and is running Peter Shor's calculations!

Then, pause... then quantum computers be able to access my private data? This is a problem.

Do not stress that the fact that classical cryptography isn't completely threatened. Although certain aspects of the classical cryptography system could be impacted due to quantum computers, quantum mechanics incorporates a different kind of extremely secure cryptography.

What about taking look at a typical cryptographic convention known as the one-time cushion. Say that party A and party B (how would we describe them? Alice or Bob) have a long string of random zeros and ones, the mystery key. Whatever time they use this key for once, and they are the only ones to have access to the key, they could send a mysterious message in the hope that nobody else (we'll refer to her as Eve) has the chance to comprehend the message. The main issue with the one-time cushion is the actual distribution of the key. Prior to that, governments would send individuals to exchange books containing inconsistencies to use as keys. This, of course, is not true and is a complete flop. This is where quantum mechanics can be useful in the form of: Quantum Key Distribution (QKD) analyzes the distribution of totally random keys that are a bit from.

What is the way quantum mechanics be used to create these extremely-mysterious keys?

Quantum key distribution relies on a fascinating feature in quantum mechanics. any attempt to study or evaluate the quantum framework is likely to disrupt it.

It is believed that the Institute for Quantum Computing (IQC) is home to one of the very few QKD models that exist on the planet. "Alice," a gadget located at the IQC home office, receives one-half of the captured (exceptionally related) photon pair that is produced by a laser placed on surface of the structure in the University of Waterloo. "Bounce" is housed at the nearby Perimeter

Institute, and gets another portion of captured photons.

Photons possess a unique characteristic that is quantifiable called the polarization (which is a sound that should be recognizable to any savviest of hues).

Because the polarization of each photon is completely random It is very unlikely to know the unique properties of each photon prior to the time. In any event, this is where entrapment becomes fascinating: if Alice and Bob analyze the polarizations of the captured photons they receive, their results are the same (recollect, "entrapped" signifies that the particles are remarkably aligned with each other even over long distances). Based on the polarization of each image, Alice and Bob attribute either "one" or a "zero" to each photon they receive. This way If Alice receives a string such as 010110 Bob also receives a 010110. However, if, for instance the case, there is a busybody trying to observe the message.

The framework will be affected which will cause a disruption to the framework. Alice Bob and Alice Bob will get a rapid notice that their keys do not co-ordinate.

Alice Bob and Bob continue to receive photos until their keys are long enough and undistinguishable enough that suddenly, they've got super-secure keys for encryption of correspondences.

In the quantum world, you could break codes and create them. What else?

Bounty. Quantum computers have the ability to create quantum frameworks that are productively reproduced this is something that physicist Richard Feynman suggested in 1982, which was a success and launched the field. Quantum frameworks can be recreated is described as an "sacred goal" of quantum computing. It will allow us to look at, in an astonishing detail communications between particles and iotas. This can help us in developing new drugs and materials, like superconductors operating at the temperature of ambient. One of the other tasks for which quantum computers are invariably faster than conventional computers is to look through an array of possible options for the optimal arrangement. Researchers are always trying out innovative quantum techniques and programs. But the true power of quantum computers has probably not been imagined at this time. The creators of the laser no doubt did not envision supermarket checkout scanners or CD players, as well as eye medical procedures. Furthermore, the future uses for quantum computer are influenced to a particular an imaginative mind.

Sounds extraordinary! I wonder where to buy quantum computers?

One second. Although quantum computing has been shown to possess a colossal potential, and researchers have been working in IQC and across the world to discover the potential of quantum computers however, there's plenty of work to be completed before quantum computers can be introduced to the market.

What are the prerequisites to build quantum computers?

We need qubits which behave they are supposed to. They could be composed of photons, iotas particles, or electrons, or something else. Researchers at IQC are examining an enormous collection of qubits as possible sources to build quantum computer. But, as it happens qubits are notoriously difficult to regulate, as any disruption causes them to drop out of quantum states (or "decohere"). Decoherence can be described as the Achilles' factor of quantum computing but it's not a bad thing. The area of quantum mistake correction studies ways to combat decoherence and combat various blunders. In constant research, scientists at IQC and all over the world are identifying better ways to let qubits take part.

When will we see an actual quantum computer?

It is based on your definition. Quantum computers exist currently, however, they are not enough to compete with classical computers. Researchers of IQC and MIT hold the ebb flow record in the world for the largest amount of qubits that were used in a test (12). While quantum advancements are increasing -- with highly effective sensors, actuators and various gadgets the quantum computer that can beat conventional computers is some time away. Theorists are always trying to find the meaning of more effective methods to overcome the decoherence problem, while researchers have gained in control over quantum technology by utilizing various advances and tools. The most important work that is being conducted now is getting ready for the quantum era that is coming.

Quantum technology is many years away?

Quantum innovations are not in use at present! QKD is now economically accessible and is expected to make huge profits through recent discoveries (scientists working at IQC are currently searching for quantum encryption using the free space of satellites). Although a fully functioning quantum computer is a longer long-term goal many significant and common sense discoveries have been made for purpose the advancement of quantum computation. The quantum sensors as well as actuators allow researchers to study the nano-scale world with incredible accuracy and sensitivity. These devices will be crucial to the advancement of true quantum processors for data.

The quantum revolution is underway and the possible possibilities that are ahead are endless.

Chapter 2: Are Quantum Computers a Reality or Just a Scientists Dream?

Are Quantum Computers a Reality or Just a Scientists Wet Dream? The quick answer to that question is yes! Quantum Computers are a reality however, they're not quite that far off from the norm yet.

Did you see the movie Iron Man and his talking computer, which is also a thinking machine as well as Terminator, the spirit-filled robot have you seen it yet? Why shouldn't we talk about a book that depicts an anecdotal invention that exceeds the current level of knowledge?

If you've seen it the ability to see, then you're directly considering that the current processing speeds of our fastest computers will not be as fast as what you've experienced. There is a possibility that if we had enough computational force we can create a copycat of insight, (This is my favored representation of man-made consciousness. I believe that we can not ever create computer-generated thinking that is able to think, feel and is aware of itself. Scientists will convince you that this is possible that in some way or another, in the event you can gather enough force for preparation in a single device, it will in all likelihood, just like enchantment be aware of its own).

In the end, it is impossible to create a device that would test an unlimited measurement of power handling. because it will without likely fail on numerous occasions due to keeping device cool and running for long enough to measure the properties it has, and even with the current processors' size breaking records for shrinking in size at all likelihood require a lot of these to provide an research team a chance to earn money.

Quantum Processors offer expectation and they're coming to us sooner, not the future, as I've stated for computers that have a spirit of the need of a more notable and random science. However, it is for computing devices that provide unlimited power for preparing and will not suffer from the negative consequences of slowing downtimes with graphic applications such as gaming consoles or require time to render data from an explosion star.

In June 2009, scientists from Yale University made a Solid State Quantum Processor! A processor that utilizes quantum laws Quantum Physics to figure, instead of 0's or 1's. The processor has recently demonstrated that it is feasible to develop such a device but is still in its early stages and does not have any down to practical usage. It does, however, answer the question in the title by saying YES!

I'm not going to attempt to clarify Quantum Physics in this article It would be more beneficial in the event you have read a book on this subject. It is ideal to comment on this article, I'm guessing that you'll find it confusing. As it is, explain the crucial difference between the Quantum Processor and a lowland regular dependable Intel Processor.

It is possible that the Intel Processor will register an issue with 1's and zero's which means "On, Off. Solids say that it is the Intel Processor needs to glance through a wide array types of Social Security Numbers, after you enter your personal Social Security Number for a match.

It is the Intel Processor will go down the list in a series until it finds an appropriate match or reaches the top of the listing. It is a tedious process and larger lists will start to reveal the cutoffs that the processor has reached.

The Quantum Processor is in a superior place over a conventional Processor similar to the one mentioned above. Based on Quantum Physics and the Laws of Quantum Physics the Quantum Processor can check the entire list like it were only checking just one Social Security Number. At the end of the day, it is clear that the Quantum Processor, can figure with no real break points in its speed.

Quantum Processor Quantum Processor would set aside an identical effort to create an inventory with 100000 Social Security numbers as it takes to create the list with only the one Social Security number!

Chapter 3: Why Quantum Computing?

Quantum Mechanics (QM) portrays the behavior and properties of elementary particles, such as such as photons or electrons at the subatomic and nuclear levels. The term was coined in the first half of the 20th century by Schrodinger [Sch26Schrodinger], Bohr [Boh08], Heisenberg [Casand Dirac [Dir95The only time in the latter part of the 70's when quantum data handling frameworks had been suggested [Pop75] Ing76, Man80]. In the 1980's of the sole remaining centuries , it was Feynman who proposed the initial physical recognition of the Quantum Computer Fey85. As a corollary the work of Feynman, Benioff [Ben82] was also among the principal researchers to discover the principles of quantum computing and Deutsch suggested the primary Quantum Algorithm [Deu85]. The reason these concepts occur due to the enthusiasm of computers designing networks is due to Moore's law [Moo65] the number of transistors on an electronic chip pair like clockwork and the dimensions of entryways is constantly shrinking. This means that issues, such as heat dissipation, data issues are growing more important in the near future and for the present. The increase in dimensions of transistors ultimately leads to the development of a technology that takes a look at the rudimentary level of particles, like one electron or photon. Since Moore's paper, this advancement has led to the current 35 nm (3.5 /10-10m) circuit technology, which thinks regarding the dimension of an one iota (roughly 10- 10m) is usually close to nuclear size. This is why the research of QM and the associated Quantum Computing turns out to be crucial for the improvement of the technology's logic structure and ultimately to the advancement in quantum algorithmic algorithms, quantum CAD, quantum logic synthesis, engineering systems and theories. Due to their widespread display and their explicit issue-related characteristics, quantum computers will be utilized for the most extensive purposes in mechanical technology and computational insights as compared to traditional type computers, they will finally become a part of every technology and daily life.

Regardless of that it is based on dumbfounding standard, QM has discovered applications across all areas of technology and logical research. But the most important potential and further practical advances were made in the area of Quantum computing quantum data, quantum computing and quantum circuits (BBC+ 95 and SD96[BBC+ 95, SD96].

Although only speculative ideas about the use of quantum computers in complete designs have been suggested (BBC+95, Fey85 Ben82, and Deu85],, the constant advancements in technology will allow the creation of Quantum Computers in close future possibly in the next 10 to 50 years from 10-50 years. The constant advancement of technology and designs show that this area is in its early stages and is expanding. For instance, the implementation of small quantum logic shows lots of molecules that have been caught or particles [BBC+95], NC00, CZ95 DKK03 PW02] are the evidence that the amount of time in the in the near future may be diminished to just a couple of years prior to the first fully quantum computer is created. The most innovative use of quantum computers is the adiabatic computer DWAVE [AOR+02, AS04, vdPIG+06, HJL+10, ALT08AOR+ 02, AS04, vdPIG+ 06, HJL. Despite the fact that it's still unanswered about whether DWAVE computer is a proper quantum-computer or nothowever, it provides a substantial acceleration over traditional computers in SAT execution as well as in it's Random Number Generation []. As a quantum computer that is adiabatic models for quantum computers have been suggested [MOC02], SO02, MOC02, SO02. These models claim that quantum calculations are performed with a number of flying photons that indicate the amount of potential for connections between qubits. The models, however, have not been implemented as of yet.

This chapter outlines the key notions of quantum computing because of the shift from quantum science and technology to quantum computer. We also provide quantum computing models that are essential to understand our concepts of quantum computing, quantum logic and the synthesis in quantum logic circuits.

Chapter 4: How Quantum Computers Will Work

Quantum computers offer a second time for speedy calculations. They'll be several times faster than the current silicon-based computers. The current fast computer in front of you is basically the same as its 30 ton predecessors, which were equipped with more than one-hundred vacuum tubes, and nearly 805 km (500 miles) of wire!

Moore's law:

When the year was 1965 Intel principal supporter Gordon Moore predicted what was to come. Moore's forecast, popularly referred to by the name Moore's Law, expresses that the amount of transistors in the chip will change regularly. This notion of silicon mix, brought into fact by Intel which has driven the technology's overall transformation.

In a quantum computing system, the data unit that is the basis (called the quantum bit, or qubit) is not coupled with each other, but is progressively quantum in the natural world.

The qubit's property is the direct result of its conformity to the quantum mechanics laws that are fundamentally different with the rules of traditional material science. Qubits may exist not only in a condition which is comparable against the coherence state of 0 or 1 in the traditional piece, but also in states that relate to superposition or a mixture of these traditional states.

Quantum energy is intense.

Computers:

As technology develops it is collaborating with a handful of components to help us move towards quantum computing, pushing out old-fashioned silicon-based chips. These components are increasing in size, utilization of vitality as well as the financial aspect of building drive At the rate of chips reduction, vitality efficiency and financial issues the typical computing device of 2020 (on the chance it is possible to achieve it through any means) could include the CPU operating with a speed of 40 GHz (or 40,400 milliseconds) that would have 160GB (160,000 millibytes) of random access memory (RAM) and operate with 40 watts of power.

Scaling: The computer world is full of innovations and massive numbers of them are comprised of smaller and more powerful chips. Chip limits have increased every an year for a year-and-a-half according to Moore's Law, however, the size of chips remains constant. The amount of transistors on one chip is increasing exponentially. It is believed that if scaling down continues at the current pace that a chip is being spoken to by one particle continuously for 2020.

Future Computers:

Particles Packed In An "Egg Carton" Of Light?

Researchers from Ohio State University have stepped towards the development of incredible new computers by revealing tiny gaps that are not a problem in any way imagination.

The openings, dim spots inside an egg made of laser light could one day to today support molecules that are used that are used in quantum computing

Central confinement to quantum computers

Quantum computers that store information in quantum bits (or qubits) will be able to stand up to a major obstacle. This is the claim that was made by Dutch hypothetical physicists of The Foundation for Fundamental Research on Matter (FOM).

Obstructions and Research:

The researchers stated that the possibilities for quantum computing is huge and that the pace of advancement has given us a new way to think - but there are many barriers to be overcome prior to quantum computers becoming economically feasible. For them to be useful quantum computers will require at least a couple of dozen qubits in order to be able to solve real issues.

In the present, studies are underway to find methods to counteract the risky consequences of decoherence in order to build the ideal engineering plan for the construction of quantum computers as well as to discover quantum algorithms that can make use of the enormous computing power that is available in these devices. The majority of the time, this fascination is connected to quantum blunder repair algorithms and quantum code.

Chapter 5: The Future Is Quantum

Quantum appears to be an extension of the possibilities and what's probable. It is the basis of sci-fi science fact and is present. In all likelihood, it's now. Quantum computing has baffled researchers for over three years, and now it appears that we're only two short years away from having them in our local technology stores.

What's the big deal with quantum computers in any way? In the end, they're super-fast and extremely efficient, making modern computers resemble the massive computers that filled a huge area when they first developed. According to Fred Chong, from the University to California quantum computers could be able to resolve problems in months that aren't important that would require a conventional computer many years.

The path towards the quantum bits "superness" is the way qubits or quantum bits aren't bound by the real-world events that we are likely to see that they have. Normal electrons rotate clockwise or counterclockwise. Quantum electrons can turn in two directions without delay. The ability to transcend the solitary reality suggests that when they're used to compute, quantum electrons transform normal "bits" into qubits. Bits that are regular can be one or zero but qubits may be both.

In terms of quantum mechanics the qubits are in superposition. This causes an inherent parallelism that according to the physicist David Deutsch permits quantum computers to attempt one million calculations without even a second's delay. The current PCs are capable of chipping away at only one.

One of the major advantages of quantum computers in addition to the numerous "superness", is that they'll render silicon-based microchips that are out of date. This is something to be grateful for considering the fact that in about four years, silicon chips have been able to outgrow their existence, and will be too small to even consider being useful in any way.

One way in that silicon chips will be discredited and completely disrupt the way that computers are wired by using the quantum property of Teleportation. By teleportation, information around one molecule can be transferred to another without using any wires in any way. To put it in Star Trek terms, data is shot beginning with one molecule and then on to the next. The nice aspect of quantum is the fact that it will always be enough capacity to accomplish this. There's no fumbling around in space, or worrying at the thought of another Klingon attack for these babies. You're always good to go.

Simple quantum computers are currently available, but they're still not close to realizing what they're capable of accomplish. In 2007 an Canadian group, D-Wave, made a 16-qubit (the aim is, at a minimum, thirty Qubits) quantum computer which could solve

Sudoku puzzles. Other quantum computers could solve the Schrodinger's cat (a feline inside the form of a poisoned container is it dead or alive? When you take the container open and discover that it has two states, comparable to qubits and quantum electrons) It was thought to be as one of the most significant aspects of quantum mechanics.

Quantum Mechanics To Interpret Or Not To Interpret

Quantum theory can be described as, of foremost importance, a vastly improved mathematical apparatus that operates.

The science behind this progressive theory was developed from an urgent desire to control scientific equipment and to transmit information on test systems with explicit tests. As the most scientifically sound theory, quantum theory requires no ontological knowledge. The most educated professionals do not even consider ontological arguments as legitimate.

Philosophical Differences

Cosmology is the study of the nature of. Epistemology is an investigation into what we know.

Metaphysics operates on the idea that there is an existence that we are currently that is being investigated. Epistemology, however, doubts the existence of anything and is only a matter of watching it in clear terms. Quantum theory is, in this way, is epistemology's embodiment as physicists that apply it for all purposes and purposes allow a negative scenario for ontological doubts regarding the existence of genuine objects before the perceptions and estimates.

In the conventional way that the majority of physicists utilize quantum theories, perceptions and estimates are the primary routes to actual information. Any information that isn't able to be observed and evaluate in terms of quantum in this way is not real. In the event that we only watch chances of being able to watch certain occasions then the only thing we can claim on the subject is only as much as these possibilities. Any additional hypotheses are bogus.

The State Of Reality

The most cutting-edge scientific notion regarding "the truth" is on very unstable grounds, because the current science theories have strayed away from human observations that have always provided significance to our physical world. Some people might say that the current notion about "the truth" is in an unsatisfactory state. Quantum physicists will declare this to be an unscientific conclusion and acquiesce their precise scientific "state vector" as the primary conceivable representation of the actual world.

This dedication to numerical strategies can be a frightening thought for those who are accustomed to creative perspectives. Precision in science however, the case, is a boon only for the numerical creative minds, which are similar to other creative thinker's mind, but only in the specialists who have succeeded in math's various patterns. But, the it isn't as wide-ranging as an artistic creative mind. This is, as I understand, the basis of all debates concerning how to comprehend quantum math. The majority of people who are arguing over the meaning of quantum math aren't math-savvy however, they are looking for an unscientific resonance with mathematicians, regardless and I think that this is a reasonable goal.

The Real Argument

I could even admit that there is any scientifically valid argument regarding what is the "best translation" of quantum theory. When I say "understanding," I signify "ontological translation." The theory clearly incorporates a variety of ontological concepts. Discussions about ontological understandings at this stage, are merely fashion-forward arguments and tasty contentions. They are legitimate in their particular domains (i.e. expressions of human experience).

Why are there so many heated arguments about the "best translation" of quantum mechanics?

The answer to this question is that humans generally require more than just precise devices to live a meaningful life. We require a sacramental vision to wrap our precise perceptions. We need a wider viewpoint to protect the anatomical and physiological structure. We require a logical interaction between tactile discernments and imaginable strategies. A similar interface is definitely stylish, given that we discover our most significant sources of inspiration in the object's or a thought's aesthetic appeal.

Even science has the ability to be a fitting fit to the most notable culture which it's placed. Science theories are, therefore, aren't able to escape the possibility of becoming trendy or trendy.

The Adiabatic Quantum Computing Model

The quantum computing model adiabatic was developed at the time of 2000 Farhi and co. [145] who proposed the use of a mathematical formula to solve advance problems, such as SATISFIABILITY (SAT) There is evidence that suggests this calculation omits an exponential amount of effort for a handful of (nondeterministic polynomial-time) problem that are NP-complete. The enthusiasm for quantum computing adiabatic model was revived in 2005, when Aharonov and colleagues. showed that it is similar as the quantum circuit.

An adiabatic process is a semi-static process in thermodynamics where no heat is transferred in a way that is different from an adiabatic system is that it is an isothermal process where the warmth is transferred in order to hold the temperature constant. A adiabatic progression in a quantum frame suggests that the Hamiltonian is changing gradually as described in Section 1.6 which explains how the Hamiltonian administrator compares with the complete vitality of the quantum frame. The Hamiltonian is an Hermitian administrator and its eigenvector which compares to the smallest value (i.e. it is the lowest level of complete dynamic that the framework has) is called the foundational state that the structure. A neighborhood Hamiltonian is an quantum framework, where the connections are made only between the same, but rather small amount of particles.

The adiabatic estimate is a well-known method to derive a surmised answer for the Schrodinger problem in the event that the Hamiltonian is slowly changing. This technique is based on a simple idea that if you have the quantum framework constructed in a ground state , and the Hamiltonian is not changing in a slow enough manner to the point that in the long run the structure will remain in a location that is near the condition of the current Hamiltonian. This is the thought that is captured by the adiabatic theory from Born as well as Fock.

A solid framework remains in its immediate eigenstate when it follows up with it in a gradual manner and if there's an in-between between the Eigenvalues (comparing to this Eigenstate) as well as the rest of Hamiltonian's range.

Think about a quantum framework that is that is in the state ps(t)>, Hn and a Hamiltonian H(t). The Schrodinger condition demonstrates the growth of the framework

iddt|ps(t)> =H(t)|ps(t)>

Accept the fact that Hamiltonian H(t) is changing slowly:

H(t)=H~(t/T),

in which T regulates the rate of the variety of H(t) as well as H~(t/T) can be found in a smooth one-parameter set consisting of Hamiltonians, H~(s), zero s= 1. The immediate eigenstates I; s>, and eigenvalues, Ei that are derived from H~(s) are described as

H(s)|i;s> =Ei|i;s>

The eigenvalues for H~(s) are required.

E0(s)<=E1(s)<=... <=En(s)

calls i=0;s = 0> , the ground area for H~(0). The adiabatic hypothesis states that if the gap between the minimum Vitality Levels E1(s) E1(s) - E0(s) is 0 . <= 1, at that point the state, | ps(t)> in the framework, following an improvement as portrayed through the Schrodinger condition is close to the ground-state that is the case for that Hamiltonian H(t) in the case of zero = t= T when T is large enough.

The adiabatic quantum computing system moves between an initial state that is the Hamiltonian Hint state and the final state using the Hamiltonian Final. The information information and the computation are stored as the ground territory of Hint and the result to the calculations is that it is now the ground region of Hfinal. The duration of the adiabatic computation can be determined by the tiny hole in the otherworldly structure in all Hamiltonians within the structural structure.

H(s)=(1-s)Hinit+sHffina[,0<=s<=1

This is because Hamiltonians rest upon the straight line connecting Hint and Hfinal[33. The base condition of the Hamiltonian Hfinal to be used in improvements calculated in the [145] formula was an old-fashioned described in the computational basis in addition, Hfinal was a corner-to- corner lattice, which was the result of the arrangement that was a combination enhancement question. This limitation was removed by Aharonov and co. This requires to have the Hamiltonians be located in the same neighboring. This assumption is similar to one that is imposed on the quantum circuit model. The quantum circuit model must be specific, that quantum doors function with a constant number of qubits.

Quantum Logic

Logic minimization is a dazzling field of computer development as well as in the present book, a variety of emerging research perspectives related to the robotized synthesis, search, and the minimization of quantum circuits will be described. The book discusses Quantum Logic Synthesis, the methods used are easily defined by the depictions which are used. Different methods are employed when orchestrating FSM's Logic Circuits, Behaviors or Quantum Cellular Automata. In evolutionary methods, for instance that combine an FSM with a developmental approach is the most prominent strategy. includes the Genetic Programming [Koz92, Koz94] whereas the synthesis of Boolean circuits or logic capacities is mostly accomplished using The Genetic Algorithm. Algorithmic techniques, for example, structure or otherworldly synthesis [SBM05a,SBM05b,Mil02,MMD06,PARK+01,KPK02,GAJ06,FTR07,WGMD09, SZSS10, PLKK10] have been utilized also.

In this section , we present concepts that can be used to synthesise quantum logic for quantum natives as well as their cost. We describe a general approach to synthesize quantum circuits. Different heuristics will be examined at a utilitarian level, in order to demonstrate the logic synthesis methods used in Machine Learning (Chapter ??). The ideas presented are the cost of quantum entrances used in our synthesis strategies and we specifically look at the quantum inductive influence on an algorithm for synthesising logic which could be used in conducting robot control by using inductive AI.

Research conducted on the robotized quantum circuits and the synthesis of them

The need for smaller cost, more economical and perfect circuits in the area of quantum logic and reversed logic has led to numerous circuits and entryways that are typically used as all-inclusive, tiny natives of logic synthesis (BBC+ 95 Per00, SD96, the HSY+ 04]. There are several features being searched for, and some of them are completeness, low realization cost as well as technology specificity and outstanding properties of synthesis. The general target is a summation of the sub-objectives mentioned with different levels of importance for each of these targets. But dependent on the multi-faceted nature of the problem also, it is necessary to pinpoint the specific goals of the fractional and study each one on its own.

It was discovered by [DiV95], DiV95 SD96, MML+98 Per00 that doors (quantum circuits) with more than one qubit can be assembled using only one qubit and select two-qubit natives. One of the most significant tests is to create the most essential doors that could be used, such as, Fredkin [SD96, LPG+04 or Toffoli that have the lowest price for the technology chosen. As illustrated by the description of quantum logic , Chapter 1. the unmistakably quantum logic synthesis is the process of identifying patterns of doorways that are crude with the aim of ensuring that their resulting lattice is comparable to the unitary network.

The issue is apparent in a similar way to planning traditional logic circuits using basic logic doors using an in particular form of the Karnaugh Map (KMap) [DM94]. In [LPG+04] the synthesis process of quantum circuits is non-monotonic starches, which makes it difficult to apply robotic systems for quantum circuit synthesis , without relying on specific methods. Furthermore, as observed from matrices that speak of entryways or circuits their dimension increases exponentially as the number of qubits.

For example, a circuit that has 3 qubits is communicated to by an array which is of size 23 by 23 (64 components) and a circuit that has five qubits will be able to form the size of a lattice that is 25x25 (1024 elements). Every element of this lattice is it is a complex number and the number of components in the network might even require an exponential time. Additionally that, in quantum logic synthesis, all circuits are able to be built from multiple perspectives by using quantum doors, without the need for additional qubits. In it's end, any circuit that is created by a unitary change U, is able to be recognized by a set number of doors or be recognized in infinitely many circuits with different prices; the more entrances to the circuit that are available in the information set the greater the possibilities for synthesizing process are feasible. In this way, the issue of reduction in Quantum Logic Synthesis is not only an issue of growing exponentially the area of arrangement in the dimensions of the circuit but it is also about discovering the tiny door arrangement that could allow a conceivably small arrangement.

There are no prerequisites, and the synthesis problem that was discussed in the previous passage is NP. The way to orchestrate a circuit using quantum entryways can be seen as a Subset Entirety (rucksack) [GJ79, CLRS01]. To comprehend this, you need to think about an underlying dimensions arrangement of quantum entranceways and then determine whether there exists a circuit that has doors that can execute capacity of f? This scenario is almost identical to the Knapsack problem. In particular, relying on technology, the goal is to construct a general entrance using just one-qubit or two-qubit natives.

The majority of the realized quantum circuits synthesis methods are for just a only a few qubits, or for only a few doors, or for specific obliged logic groups of capabilities, (for example, reversible or direct capacities). The most widely recognized Quantum Logic Synthesis (QLS) approaches are utilized for the plan of simply quantum permutative (reversible) logic circuits [MD03,LPG+ 04,LP02,YHSP05,YSPH05, MDM05, SBM05a, SBM05b, MDM07, HSY+ 06, WGMD09, PLKK10, ?]. The synthesis of reversed circuits could also split into two distinct subcategories. One method to handle the reversible logic configuration is to rely extensively on the utilization of ancilla bits (MD03, MDM05, WGMD09and the second one builds reversible logic circuits only on the tiny amount of qubits [MP02 LPG+04; YHSP05; FTR07, ?, and LSKed]. The common method of separating the two types of reversible synthesizing logic is the fact that the countless qubits of ancilla can possibly reduce the amount of pathways to join the circuit, but at the expense of ancilla bits [MWD10and [MWD10].

A more extensive QLS for quantum circuits with discretion was constructed using a smaller number of qubits [Yab00 and Rub01; LPG+03 and LSKed[Yab00, Rub01, LPG+03, LSKed. This method has been ultimately tested progressively until now due to the fact that there's likely to be an inexplicably large quantity of quantum entrances which could be used in the QLS. In these methods, a single calculation - a genetic calculation was employed to create or improve quantum circuits.

Therefore, despite some results previously reported of the QLS method, there isn't a way to create a system that can orchestrate more than two qubit quantum circuits using quantum non-permutative natives. Some of the methods are adapted from Reversible logic synthesizing and are utilized mostly for synthesis using the CNT entranceways (NOT, Feynman and Toffoli) or similar libraries, which do not allow the full power of quantum circuits as well as quantum logic. There is also a small collection of other libraries of doors to quantum logic synthesizing [BBC+ 95 SD96, SD96, YSPH05, LP02 LPK10[BBC+ 95, SD96, YSPH05, LP02].

In addition, there are methods using the presumed multi-controlled Toffoli (MCT) doors as unique part-door synthesis [MMD03 MDM05, MDM07, WGMD09 and PLKK10], where the capacity arranged into a circuit dependent on Toffoli doors. A closer match to quantum equipment use is, for instance, the approach that was proposed in [SBM05a] and the building of the reversible door is completed using the alleged quantum multiplexer. However, there is no proof that any one of them have the negligible quantum acknowledgment cost for every circuit that may utilized for the decision. In this regard, it is still an open question to find the entryways that allow for the creation of a less excessive circuit (in the number of doors and the amount of accessories) to accommodate different technological advancements.

Quantum Advantage

Quantum Advantage achievement Quantum Advantage achievement accept explicit quantum calculation benchmarks43 that be unable to reproduce on conventional computers. Google has recently offered such benchmarks to address particular issues and has been pushing for real upgrades to the reenactment algorithm.

In a sign of this that they have found a number of escape clauses in benchmarks, which make reproducing them much easier. The escape clauses were removed at the time Google released revised benchmarks.

Once all is said and completed, we expect that there will be a period of mouse and feline as escape clauses increase and then close to quantum advantages benchmarks.

For instance, the groupings of doors that are corner to corner must be maintained at an appropriate distance from each other because they enable efficient tensor-organize compression strategies.

The estimations based on computation applied to corner entryways could also be used in a way that is not intended.

Sometimes the escape clauses come with characteristics that can be checked using confirmation strategies.

Scientists Hint at Smartphone - Sized Quantum Computers

Researchers say cell phone-measured quantum computers may be built by using particles and microwaves, pointing to the possibility of smaller quantum computing devices in the near future.

Physics researchers at NIST's National Institute of Standards and Technology (NIST) have been able to connect their quantum property of two distinct particles through the use of microwaves instead of the usual laser bars.

The researchers suggest that it is possible to replace a vibrant space-sized quantum computing "laser park" with scaled-down technology, such as business microwaves, those used in advanced cells.

"It's possible an unobtrusive estimated quantum computer could inevitably seem as though an advanced mobile phone joined with a laser pointer-like gadget, while sophisticated machines may have a general impression practically identical to a standard work area PC," claims NIST scientist Dietrich Leibfried.

Scientists have stated that microwave components could be expanded and upgraded in a way that is more effective to create down-to-earth frameworks that contain thousands of particles to enable quantum computation and replication as opposed to the awe-inspiring, expensive laser sources.

While microwaves, which are the main source of correspondence between distant locations were used before to in the control of single particles, NIST researchers were the first place microwave sources that are close to particles that are only 30 micrometers away, and create the conditions that allow for ensnaring.

The snare is a quantum phenomenon that is expected to be crucial to transmitting data and rectifying mistakes within quantum computer.

Scientists have integrated microwave sources simply in a particle trap that was chip-sized and created a that is a scale table of mirrors, lasers and focal point that is about one-tenth the size that was previously needed. Although low-power bright lasers are not yet anticipated to cool particles and allow for the observation of exploratory results however, they could be the case that they will eventually be reduced to as small as the ones found in DVD players.

"Even though quantum computers are not thought of as comfort gadgets that everyone needs to haul around, they could utilize microwave hardware like what is utilized in PDAs. These parts are very much produced for a mass-market to help advancement and diminish costs. The possibility energizes us," Leibfried said.

Particles offer the best chance for quantum bits, also known as qubits to store information in a quantum computer. While another potential candidate for qubits is superconducting circuits that are extremely efficient, which are also known as "counterfeit molecules"- are controlled by chips using microwaves quantum qubits, particles are at an even further stage of development because more particles are able to be controlled with greater accuracy and with less losses of information.

The most recently conducted tests in the most recent trials, the NIST team used microwaves to move in the "turns" of individual magnesium particles as well as capture the twists of a handful of particles. It's an "all-inclusive" arrangement of quantum logic because revolutions and snare are able to be combined together to perform every quantum computation that is allowed by quantum mechanics Leibfried declares.

In the experiments, the two particles were captured by electromagnetic fields floating over the particle trap chip made of gold terminals that were electroplated onto an aluminum-nitride back. A part of the anodes were activated to produce waves of radio waves around the particles. The frequencies of radiation are within range of 1 to 2 gigahertz region.

The microwaves create beautiful fields that turn the twists of particles that could be thought of as tiny bar magnets that point in different ways. The direction these tiny bar magnets is one the quantum properties that communicate to information.

Scientists captured the particles through changing a method they invented using lasers. If the microwaves' magnetic fields are able to step in a step on the particle in a optimal manner, the particles' movements can be activated depending on the direction of the turn and twists. The particles could be captured all the time.

Scientists had to find the right combination of parameters in the three cathodes, which would give an optimal variation in tilting fields of attraction depending on the extent of the particle's movement, while limiting unwanted impact. The characteristics of the particles that are snared are interconnected in order that the measurement of one particle will reveal the state of the other.

Quantum computers are gadget that calculates using quantum mechanical marvels, for instance, superposition and snare to perform actions using the data. The fundamental principle behind quantum computation is that the quantum property are able to communicate and report information, and execute operations with this data.

Quantum computers could be able to use with the baffling rules of quantum material sciences to address specific problems such as breaking the current most commonly used encryption algorithms for information that are currently remain inaccessible even with supercomputers.

A more specific goal is to design quantum replicas of major scientific challenges and to study quantum puzzles, like superconductivity at high temperature, elimination of resistance to electrical energy specific materials when properly chilled.

Researchers have concluded that the use of microwaves can reduce the blunders caused by uncertainties in laser shaft pointing and power , as well because lasers trigger unconstrained emission by the particles. In any case microwave-related tasks must be enhanced to enable functional quantum calculations, or reproductions.

Is Quantum Computing Closer Than We Thought?

Quantum computing may be able to prepare improved technology for computers in the near future. It's evident that silicon is approaching its limits for its use in microprocessors'. So what kind of advances would be possible to achieve, and could they be said to be more near than we anticipated?

The most talked about topic you'll hear about regarding the next generation of processors and technology is the term 'quantum computing'. Presently, processors use two-fold code made up of 0's and 1's in order to follow guidelines encode, interpret, and count. Quantum technology could alter the way we use technology today. The quantum computing theory is to regulate the movement of electrons (quantum particles) which means that electrons can be moved in two different bearings similar to with the vague turn positions called quantum states. The electron can communicate with either '1', or '0 simultaneously and is the foundation for the potential power that a quantum computer can provide.

Additionally, when quantum processors store the data by storing it in qubits astonishingly - it will then be able to master this data in order to get every result that is possible. The power a quantum processor might provide could be beneficial to computers, but perhaps it could help us in developing future medical and scientific advancements more quickly than ever before? since the current silicon-based processors lack the force, speed, and accuracy to analyze the many facets of particle.

Qubits and Quantum Memory

In the old-fashioned method of calculation data, the unit is a single piece of data, which could be either 0 or. Quantum computation it is called quantum bits (qubit) that is the result of superposition between the numbers 0 and

1. Imagine a framework having two base states, which we call the j0i and the j1i. These basis states are distinguished using the two symmetrical vectors 1and

0, separately. A single qubit may be in any superposition

0

1

0j0i + 1j1i; j 0j2 + j 1j2 = 1:

A similar way the qubits of a single qubit "live" in the C2 vector space.

In addition, there are frameworks that have more than one qubit, that live" in the tensor space of a handful of qubit frameworks. For instance two qubit frameworks have four basis states that are j0i, J0i j1i and j1i j0i. For instance, j1i j0i indicates that the first qubit exists in the foundation state j1i, while it is the 2nd qubit that's in its foundation state of j0i. It is common to reduce this to j1ij0i 1; 0i, or the j10i.

For the vast majority of the time that a register of two qubits contains 2n base expresses, all of them being jb1 I JB2I:jbni. Bi 2 f0 and 1g. It is possible to abridge this to jb1b2:bni. We often reduce 0 : 0 to 0n. Because bitstrings with lengths of nu can be viewed as whole numbers within the range between 0 and 2n1 (see the Appendix B.2) We can as well compose the base states using numbers like j0i; J1i, j2i and j2n 1i. The vector that is comparing to the n-qubit basis state jxi is the two-dimensional vector which contains a one at the x-th place and 0s in other places (here we consider x to be an entire number in the form f0 2n 1g; and we also include the instances in the vector starting at position zero). This indicates that two n-qubit basis states, jxi and Jyi, are symmetrical, I 6x= y. Another method to discover this symmetry is to use the tensor item's standards (Appendix A.6):

HXJYI = hX1JY1I

hxnjyni = hx1jy1i

$\langle hx_n | y_n \rangle$:

As $\langle hx_k | y_k \rangle = x_k \cdot y_k$ We can see that the bases states $|x\rangle$ and $|y\rangle$ will be symmetrical if there is at least only one point at where the bits of both two x and one y are in a symmetrical way.

A quantum register with nu qubits could be in any superposition

$$2^n - 1$$

$$X$$

$$0j0i + 1j1i +$$

$$+$$

$$2^n - 1j2^n - 1i;$$

$$\sum j |j|^2 = 1:$$

$$J$$

$$=0$$

In computing this on the computational foundation we can get the state $|j\rangle$i-n-bit with probability of $j |j|^2$. The initial qubit of a state

77

will differ from the projection-based estimation, which includes the two projectionors P0 = J0IH0J

I2n 1

And P1 = J1 ih1j 1 . In this case, for instance, using this

Q

Estimation of the state

p1

j0ij i+

2

j1ij

i produces result 0 having likelihood 1/3. The state at this point changes to J0ij I. Results 1 is obtained with a probability of 2/3. The state at this point becomes J1IJ I. This is also the case when estimating the first n qubits of the (n + m)qubit state within the computational base compares with the projection estimation which includes 2n projectors Pj = jjihjjl2m for the j 2 f0 and 1gn.

One of the properties that is important and can be referred to is entrapment which refers to quantum relations between the qubits. Consider, for instance, two qubit registers that are in the state of

1

1

P

j00i +

P

j11i:

2

2

These 2-qubit states are of the times referred to as ΓPR-combincs to show appreciation for Einstein, Podolsky, and Rosen who studied these states and their allegedly complex properties. The first time we look at them, neither one nor the other qubits is able to display an old-fashioned value of the j0i or j1i. However, on the chance that we take a measurement of the first qubit and observe for an j0i at that moment the whole state is smashed into J00i. Then, watching the rst qubit rapidly xes the second qubit that is secretly xed to an old-fashioned value. Since the two qubits which comprise the register may be separated and thus, this model outlines some of the distant quantum frameworks are able to demonstrate. In general, the bipartite state jI is known as snared in case that it isn't created as a tensor element J Ai j Bi in which the j Ai is located in the first space while j Bi is within the 2nd.

A comparison with older style likelihood distributions could be beneficial. Consider two likelihood spaces, A and B, the first with two possible results The second space has two million potential outcomes. A likelihood distribution for the rst space could be represented by the numbers 2n (non-negative reals that add up to 1; there are 2n degrees of possibility in this case) and a distribution of the second can be represented by 2m numbers. A proper distribution of items in the joint space could be depicted using 2n+2m numbers. However it is true that a self-assertive (non-item) distribution of the joint space is based on 2n+m real numbers, as there are two possibilities in all. Similar to a n-qubit-state that is j Ai could be represented using the 2n number (complex numbers that have squared moduli that are averaging to 1) the m-qubit states J Bi represented by 2m numbers and their tensor item j Ai bi by 2n and 2m numbers. However the self-assertive (conceivably caught) state within the joint space is represented by 2n+m numbers since it is located in a 2n+m-dimensional space. It is evident that the amount of parameters needed to describe quantum states is comparable to the amount of parameters required to depict likelihood distributions.

Also, take note of the connection to statistical independency3 among two different factors B and A and non-trapping in the state of the object j Bi. However regardless of the similarities between probabilities and amplitudes quantum states are more prevalent than distributions, since amplitudes could include negative (or even complicated) parts that could cause obstructions and or even e and ects. Amplitudes could become probabilities if they are squared. The goal in quantum computing is the use of these unique properties to create intriguing computational applications.

Another Hardware Alternative for ML and AI: Quantum Computing

Quantum computing is advancing to grow and expand, and with the announcement that is currently being made by the Vancouver quantum computing group, D-Wave, of their 2,000-qubit processor , it doesn't provide evidence of a slowing back.

D-Wave is the principal quantum computing group which has made quantum computing available to businesses for use. Quantum computing processors face a direct concurrence with the more specialized types of chips used to support Machine Learning and AI like GPUs, as well as the recently announced second-generation TPU developed by Google.

The key feature in quantum computing is the fact that it completely replaces the standard approach to computing. In reversing the conventional piece, either 0 or by a different type of data, it is able to open up to exponential estimates of potential results. The qubit may be in a superposition state in which it is not either +1 or - 1 one could say that it is both, and this is what is the reason it takes into consideration super-fast processing.

It is believed that the D-Wave quantum computers employ the process of strengthening. This is accomplished by arranging a sequence of tiny magnets that orchestrated within the basis of a matrix. Each attractive field influences on the other, and they are arranged in an arrangement that limits the amount of vitality that is thrown out in the entire field. It is at this point that it is possible to alter the appeal of the field in each magnet, with the aim that the magnets position themselves in a way that they can solve specific problems. To achieve a steady pace starting point, you begin with a high level of vitality to make it easy for the magnets move around. When you reduce your temperature, they are in lower, lower vitality levels until they have in a solid state, which is the lowest condition of vitality. This is where it's possible to study the directions of each magnet and observe the reaction to the problem. It is possible to say that D-Wave's quantum computer an instance of a basic computer that is based on the algorithms of Nature to find the form of the least vital state.

It is here that we can make the most of. This particular type of quantum computing can help with a portion of streamlining computing problems especially those that are geared to Machine Learning. A lot of Machine Learning problems can be modified to be formulated as vitality issues. This is because the D-Wave quantum computing systems are designed to assist with problems that require high-level thinking and the process of decision-making. Quantum computing takes into consideration Artificial Intelligence or AI frameworks to replicate human thinking more deeply than a traditional processor. In addition, while quantum computing is difficult to grasp but its use for Machine Learning advance technology is evidently opening new opportunities.

In the upcoming conflict between TPUs and GPUs There is a chance the quantum computer will take place to the other side of the spectrum. The most important aspect of D-Wave's quantum computing is the fact that it's not really designed to resolve every problem, however it's serving meet the same requirement in the preparing market that GPUs currently meet. Google published a research paper that reveals that there's a significant computational advantage using the quantum computer D-Wave over an older style processor. From a variety of ways, a quantum computer is able to do what to what a GPU does just faster and this time is money.

Quantum computing is advancing to expand and, with the current declaration by the Vancouver quantum computing group, D-Wave, of their 22,000 qubit processor, it doesn't suggest that they will be slowing to a lower.

D-Wave is the primary quantum computing organisation which has made quantum computing available for commercial use. Quantum computing processors are facing an immediate battle with the more specialized types of chips that are used to support Machine Learning and AI like GPUs, as well as the recently announced second-generation TPU by Google.

The key feature in quantum computing is the fact that it alters the traditional view of computing. In reversing the conventional section of 0 or 1 with a different kind of data, it allows to exponential measurements of possible results. The qubit could be in a state of superposition in which it is not +1 or -1 yet one could say it's both, and this makes use of the super-fast computation.

This is because the D-Wave quantum computers employ the method of the toughening. This is accomplished by a sequence of tiny magnets controlled by an array. Each attractive field interacts with each other, and then following that, they organize themselves into a position that reduces the amount of energy that is absorbed by the entire area. It is at this point that you can alter the appeal of the area of each magnet to ensure that the magnets are placed in a manner that helps solve specific issues. To determine a suitable speed beginning with high levels of vitality. This makes it is straightforward for magnets to turn between. As you reduce your temperature, attraction are at low and higher levels until they're in a condition of vitality. This is where it's possible to study the direction of each magnet and observe the reaction to the problem. It is possible to say that D-Wave's quantum computers are a kind of basic computer based on the nature's algorithms to decide the best design for the diminished vitality state.

This is where we are able to make a difference. This particular kind of quantum computing can be beneficial for a particular portion of streamlining computing problems specifically those geared to Machine Learning. A lot of Machine Learning problems can be modified to be formulated as vitality problems. It is believed that the D-Wave quantum computing systems are designed to aid issues that require higher levels of thinking, and then decision-making. Quantum computing is a process that uses Artificial Intelligence or AI frameworks to replicate human thinking much more closely than traditional processors. While recognizing that quantum computing is difficult to comprehend, its application for Machine Learning advance technology is clearly opening new possibilities.

In the coming conflict between GPUs and the TPUs There is a chance of quantum computing to take in the opposite direction. The primary component of D-Wave's quantum computing is the fact that it's not designed to address every problem, but it's serving meet the same demand in the market for preparing that GPUs currently meet. Google published a research study in which they discover that there's a significant computational gain with the D-Wave quantum computer instead of traditional processors. From a variety of angles quantum computers can accomplish something that to what a GPU could do, but just.

Quantum Search

As we've discussed previously, Grover's calculation simulates a search through an unorganized arrangement of $N = 2n$ items to find the most interesting part that fulfills a particular conditions. While the most effective old-fashioned calculation to inquire into the unorganized data requires $O(N)$

time11; Grover's formula executes the quest on a quantum computing device in only $O(N)$ actions, which is the quadratic speedup.

As Grover himself states that if the calculation could be executed with the limit that is $O(\lg(\lg))$ steps at this point, it would provide a calculation of BQP to solve problems with NPC. But, Grover's calculation does not provide such an approximate runtime and is an asymptotically perfect arrangement, and therefore no authoritative argument can be made regarding the relationship between the multifaceted class of nature BQP and NP depending on the presentation of Grover's calculations.

Grover's hunt algorithm is a good prelude to quantum algorithms because it demonstrates how the properties of quantum frameworks could be used to improve the runtime limitations of conventional algorithms. In order to achieve an increase in speed, Grover depends on the quantum superposition of states. Similar to others quantum algorithm,

Grover's algorithm begins by putting the machine into an identical superposition the various 2n states of the n-qubit register. Remember that this implies that there is the same amount of plenteousness as 1/2 n for every possible layout of qubits within the framework, as well as an equal probability for 1/2 N that the structure can be in one of the two states.

The potential states are related to the various possible routes in Grover's database so that, starting with the equivalent magnitudes assigned to every component of the pursuit space Each component is examined without delay as a quantum superposition and amplitudes are controlled at this point to produce an appropriate section of the database with a chance that is "at any rate" 1/2.

Alongside the superposition of state that are based on Grover's formula as well as in the majority of the quantum algorithms that make use of what's referred to as plenteousness enhancement. These algorithms exploit the properties of quantum amplitudes which separate these amplitudes from normal probabilities. The method used to implement these algorithms is through the specific shift in the time period of a single state in an quantum framework that meets some requirement, every cycle. The process of executing a stage movement of p is similar to replicating the sufficiency of the state by - 1. The sufficiency of that state is altered but the probability for being there is the same the same way as prior to (since the probability ignores the sign of abundancy). In any case the subsequent modifications made to the framework take advantage of this difference in sufficiency to pick out the condition with a different stage and eventually increase the chances for the frame to be in the state. This kind of arrangement are not possible without the amplitudes that hold any additional information with regard to the time period of the state, regardless of probability. The abundancy enhancement algorithms are unique to quantum computing because of the nature of amplitudes which does not have a simple traditional probabilities.

Simon's algorithm How does it work

If you have a capacity that is based on strings of n-bits Simon's calculation begins by introducing two registers of n-bits in the direction of 0:

|0i n |0i n

After that, you can apply the Hadamard modification onto the register of the first will get an equivalent superposition of states:

Then, the given prophet works $f(x)$ is scrutinized in both registers. The prophet's activity is performed in a single action which demonstrates the change $Of(x)$ xi $+yi =xif(x)$ (xi). The moment the prophet comes into contact with the registers of the design illustrated, the result is that there will be no change in the first register, and $f(x)$ is discarded in the second register, as $f(x)$ zero = $f(x)$:

The next register is being estimated. There are two scenarios to think about when deciding the impact of this measurement on the main register. or the XOR veil either a = 0n, or a = 0, 1n. In the event that a = 0n, then f is injective. every estimate of x corresponds to a particular type of valued f(x). This implies that the main register remains in an equivalent superposition. Despite the deliberate calculation of f(x) it is possible that x will be any string of the range 0, 1n and with similar. In the other case, if you have a value of 0, 1n then estimating the next register determines a reliable estimate of f(x) and is referred to as f(z) which limits the possibilities of estimations for this register.

According to that capacity f(x) it is two possibilities of estimating the x, with the aim that f(x) is f(z) Z and Z. The state of the primary register following the process of estimating the other is in this manner diminished to an equivalent superposition these two characteristics:

Since there will not be additional activities taking place on the following register, any further calculations will focus on the first register. The next step is to detach the data regarding a register that is currently stored in the primary register. This can be accomplished using the Hadamard change again. Keep in mind how the Hadamard change could be described by the bitwise dab x * y , which is:

By using this method, the result of applying another Hadamard process is

In this paper, the calculation of the main register has been calculated. In the ruffian scenario where A = 0. (f is injective) A string is created by 1, 0 with a the same distribution.

For the scenario where x y = 6 n , you should note that either the * y is zero or a * y = 1. In the event that * y equals 1, at this time

Condition 19f is changed to:

The sufficientness, and consequently possibility, of estimating of y will be accurate to the amount that a *y = 1 is equal to zero, therefore that y can never be calculated. Recognizing that it will always be the case that *y = 0.

Condition 19f may be separated:

At the point where 6= 0n and the repercussions of estimation of the principal register following to performing Simon's equation will create the string y 0, 1n that is: A * y = 0. Based on Equation 21a the amount of abundancy associated with each worthy y is equivalent to +2 1-n, indicating the probability:

by observing any one string y with the goal of achieving the * y is zero with a uniform distribution of 2n-1strings that satisfy * y = of 0.

In the event that Simon's calculation is run repeatedly in a row, the string n is y1 and y2 . . . , yn-1 0,1ncan be observed, which is an arrangement of n-1/1 direct conditions in n queries of the structure:

To find a solution from this is an issue of untangling the n queries each one a part of anoverall effort to come to an in general. This obviously requires the arrangement of n + 1 completely independent conditions.

The chance of seeing the principal string y0 21-n

. After another round of Simon's calculations, the probability of seeing a different piece of string would be 1 21-n . The probability of watching the n-1/1 distinct estimates of y over time which is a lower bound on the likelihood of obtaining n - 1, linearly independent equations is:

Thus, a linearly independent system of n-1/1 equations, and how much a can be determined through repeating the Simon algorithm more than 4 times. Simon's algorithm needs only O(n) inquiries to find f in order to find a, while conventional algorithms require exponential time.

Many of the more intriguing quantum algorithms, like quantum reenacted toughening, quantum reenacted symbio on the other hand , quantum Bayesian methods, demand much more thorough understanding of the basics of math. However, with the quantum worldview coming to the surface the future isn't well for quantum computation to be ignored in the computer science education for undergrads program. In the ideal scenario, research into quantum algorithms will soon become normal. At present the course will show that quantum algorithms are within the comprehension capabilities of the average computer science students, and provides a an enlightening introduction to the fundamentals of quantum computation to students who are not in the college.

Classical circuits

In the classical theory of intricacy the term "Boolean circuit" refers to the term Boolean circuit can be described as a coordinated noncyclic diagram that has AND, OR, and not doors. It is composed of two input hubs that include the n input bits (n zero). The hubs in the inner include AND, OR, and not doors. In addition, there is at least one designated yield hub. The information bits that are underlying are processed to AND, OR, and not doors, as specified by the circuit. In the end, the yield hubs will have some value. The circuit is able to process some Boolean capacity f 1gn; f0 ! 1gm if yield hubs have the right value f(x) per data 2 x 1 F0; 1gn.

Circuit families are a collection with circuits. one for each size of information (n). Each circuit is equipped with a yield bit. The family is aware of or chooses a particular language 1g; f0; [n] 1gn] if you have n infos and for each information x 1gn; the circuit Cn produces 1 if 2 L is present and returns the opposite value. This type of circuit is always polynomial if there exists an deterministic Turing machine that produces Cn when given information about n by using space logarithmic in n.1 The size (number of entries) of circuits will be able to construct any polynomial thing using an n. It is evident that always polynomial circuit families have the same capacity as polynomial-time determined Turing machines The language L could be picked by a consistently polynomial circuit group I 2 P [118], Theorem 11.5in which P is the type of dialects which can be determined by polynomial time Turing machines.

Furthermore, we can consider randomly-generated circuits. These circuits receive, in addition to the input bits n as well as random bits (\coin ips") as info. A randomized circuit registers a capacity f on the off chance that it effectively yields the correct answer f(x) with likelihood in any event 2=3 for each x (likelihood assumed control over the estimations of the irregular bits; the 2=3 might be supplanted by any 1=2 + "). Randomized circuits have the same capacity to random Turing machines. Language L could be selected by a consistent

Polynomial random circuit family I 2 BPP, in which BPP (\Bounded-blunder Probabilistic Polynomial Time") refers to the name given to the category of dialects that are detected by random Turing machines, with a progress probability in all cases 2=3.

Quantum circuits

Quantum circuits (additionally called quantum system or quantum entrance exhibit) summarizes the possibilities of classical circuit families substituting those AND, OR, and NOT doors with rudimentary quantum doors. Quantum entrances are one-time change in a small (generally 1,2 or 3) quantity of qubits. We've seen various models in the last section including the bit-ip entryway X as well as the stage ip entryway Z, and the Hadamard entrance H. The primary 2-qubit door we've seen was the controlled-NOT (CNOT) entryway. Including another control register, we get the 3-qubit Tooli entryway, additionally called controlled-controlled-not (CCNOT) door. This is in contradiction to the third part of the information in case the first two bits are one. This is the Tooli door is significant due to because it's constructed for classical reversible calculations that is, any calculation of classical origin can be accomplished via a circuit that contains Tooli entranceways. It's not hard to comprehend: by using helper wires with xed value, To oli could execute and (x the third outgoing wire to zero) and not (1) and the second wire to). It is evident that AND NOT-entryways can be used to perform every classical Boolean circuit, and in the event that we could apply (or recreate) to oli doors to execute any classic calculation in a reversed manner.

Quantitatively, these quantum doors are able to be constructed into more unitary functions by utilizing tensor items (if entryways are applied the register in different areas of the registry) as well as regular grid items (if entryways are applied in succession). We've just seen an example of basic entryways in the preceding section, and specifically for teleportation.

For instance, if you employ to the Hadamard gates H every bit of a register that contains zeroes, we get

Quantum Computing and Healthcare Technology

Imagine being able to conduct an MRI using a single cell rather than the whole body, and snapping a picture of the atom , or the particles in the phone, identifying and scrutinizing the troublesome areas inside DNAand devising an ever-more precise diagnosis and treatment. It is possible today thanks to the accuracy that is Quantum Computing and Nanotechnology incorporated with MRI hardware.

In an ongoing news release IBM announced they are extremely close to being successful in the realm in Quantum computing. Thanks to some of their exploration successes, they are getting closer to creating the initial

Quantum Computer, that can benefit from the unique properties of quantum materials science. This could allow them to solve specific problems in a matter of minutes or two, which could otherwise require computers billions of years.

Quantum computing can be described as a computer framework that is dependent on qubits, rather than bits. qubits (Quantum Bits) are the primary elements of data in quantum computers. Although a qubit can be able to speak to only two outcomes, like such as either 0 or 1, or a yes or no, Qubits can speak to several other possibilities, including 0 , 1, and 0, which is the result of various mixes of Qubits and all simultaneously. This way Qubits can speak to many possible outcomes and can be identified while simultaneously analyzing.

The Qubit concept manages tiny particle (subatomic particles). It is known that subatomic molecules can possess multiple states simultaneously due to the fact that particles are never static. This is evident on reason that they move fast, close to that speed. This is why an molecule-related condition of the quantum molecule (Qubit) is distinct to different eyewitnesses, and the molecule can be found in a number of states at any time. This is why a subatomic molecule may have a variety of states and probabilities at the same time. It is possible to use it to replace bits and display indications of improved execution. Much more efficient execution! After that after joining Qubits this blend contains an exponentially greater amount of information than bits. Subatomic logic is considerably more powerful than coupled logic that is used in normal computing.

Accordingly, you can process muddled data quicker. The primary applications of encryption are unscrambling, display, databases, voice recognition as well as structure recognition, computerized reasoning and recreation, along with a myriad of other however, there are no applications.

Consider its impact and use in the field of Healthcare specifically e-Health. Large amounts of electronic patient information, arranged in a way that can be displayed, updated and handled in fractions of seconds - human-made brainpower for diagnosis and consistency that is nearly 100% accurate is expected to increase number of creases, and outperform unconsidered areas of limitation.

Quantum Computing has additionally demonstrated that two particles that are ensnared are a part of the same. This is the moment at the moment one alters its expression while the other alters its own state simultaneously regardless of how long they have been discovered by humans. This means that we could "transport" data starting with one location and move to the next, without physical changes only by changing the state of a molecule that is caught.

In the context of e-Health, this might be a program-controlled remote and solid diagnosis using electronic patient information, via rapid communication with captured subatomic particles. In addition, with nano-scale precision technology This is just an indication of what's to come.

A New Era in Super-Computing?

If you're looking for areas where maths could be utilized to improve our current real world, look no further than computing, and in particular the most current and exciting developments coming from colleges across the US. In a meeting at the American Physical Society in Dallas researchers from the University of California, Santa Barbara have presented the most recent developments making the way for quantum computers.

Quantum computers, which currently doesn't appear to be built could be constructed to carry out calculations on a scale that can be astonished to surpass the current super-computers.

The UCSB gadget is a step in the direction of computers. It has a chip that houses nine quantum gadgets and four of them are "quantum bits" or Qubits that make the calculations. In the not too distant future, the team will plan to increase the number of Qubits to 10. When scientists are able to build the amount of Qubits to 100, they believe the chip will become the foundation of a decent and usable computer.

All of this raises the possibility that sooner and later we'll see the power of today's super-computers in our offices and on our laps even in our mobile phones.

To make these advances that we have made, we owe a large amount due to Erwin Schrodinger, whose work on quantum material science and the wave condition helped us understand the enigma in quantum mechanics.

The fundamental principle behind quantum computing is based on "super-position", which is the seemingly unnatural ability of molecules to exist in two states at once. A molecule that is turning one direction might be given a non-existent energy pulse, which might be enough to cause it to spin the opposite way but perhaps it won't. In the event that the molecule isn't being monitored or being associated in any way Quantum material science claims that the molecule can be in two states at the same time.

Now, we can utilize all of these particles to communicate with the numbers that are paired. If an estimate is made using traditional computers it is necessary to input each number in the computer in its own way. However, since quantum computers is able to work with particles that are super-positional that it is able to play out the calculation on all possible blends simultaneously. A number whose paired representation has 7 digits is within the range of 0 to 127. A standard computer will need to count each of these 127 numbers. Quantum computers could perform both at once.

In any case the power of quantum computing creates massive challenges for society. As it stands an entirely functioning quantum computer could threaten the reliability of the entire planet. It is because that global business depends on the use of secure numbers to verify and ensure financial transactions. Furthermore, many of the secure discussions between governments and other government agencies take place using similar arrangement of figures. With the incredible quantum computing capabilities that it could bring, these figures which we've considered to be invulnerable and nimble, could be useless.

The race is now ahead to see if quantum computers be the first to appear, posing threats to global security and trade? But then, could another quantum cryptography technology be developed first, which will verify transactions in a different, unbreakable manner? (It's another matter, but the possibility of such encryption was just made feasible over very short distances. It's also totally impervious to breakage.)

Limitations Of Quantum Computing

It is important to note that the quantum computing field is still in its infancy stage. Numerous constraints that are associated to it have been discovered in various trials and some of them are like this:

Quantum Decoherence

Quantum decoherence is the absence of request between the stage points typically due to the blockage of the quantum frame functioning under external impacts.The fact that quantum computers need to be isolated from other frameworks in order to function properly is an issue because isolation is extremely difficult to attain. In fact, even the appearance of a field with a wanderer can significantly affect the performance of quantum computers.

Acquiring a Valid Output

One of the major limitations of quantum computers is having a predetermined yield value which is related to the base requirements of the qubits. Structure the logical tasks that are required to achieve this is a challenge, since quantum frameworks are with a myriad of superpositions of different states at any given moment. These cannot be quantified and only the yields when comparing to the basic states can be quantified.

Numerous calculations could be done using the quantum computer before a satisfactory yield can be obtained, thereby reducing the speed of the process. The manner in which, the process of the quantum computer is monitored can alter its physical state adds to the problem.

Quantum Reenactment

Feynman's original concept of quantum computing was based on the incentive to reenact complex quantum mechanical frameworks and that's why it remains a zone of dynamic intrigue. For a considerable period of period of time, computer-generated simulations have widened our understanding of quantum mechanical frameworks but the multifaceted nature of these reenactments has forced the use of approximations which ultimately limit the amount of important data we are able to discern. The most important issue is the same certainty which makes quantum computers so compelling in that describing the quantum framework needs a variety of parameters that grow exponentially with the scale of quantum structures.

Quantum computers are able to recreate quantum mechanical frameworks across many fields such as quantum chemistry materials science as well as atomic physical sciences and even dense issue materials science.

The Boston Consulting Group has assessed that quantum reenactment that is improved could bring a market estimate of several billions to pharmaceutical companies in the simplest case.

Quantum recreating (counting the cross section of chemistry, QCD, materials science and other related fields.) is currently a significant amount of supercomputer time and we are anticipating quantum computers to not just be able to perform these games much more efficiently, but significantly expand the range of what can be achieved using them. Several quantum-based reproduction techniques have only recently been developed and tested with quantum computer. The algorithms that underlie them are developed for frameworks that use minimal resources. One promising flow direction of research is the half-quantum classical methods. These techniques offload specific calculations to classical computers, like Hamiltonian integrals could be registered using a traditional computer and later incorporated into quantum computer calculations as parameters. However quantum computers could be used to speed up fundamental parts of reenactments e.g.,giving information about 2-molecule-thickness networks.

Ground-state properties are typically discovered using variational techniques. These are techniques that iterate one selects an underlying wave work based on at least one parameter then decides on the esteem of parameters that attempt to limit normal vitality values. The next wave work is an upper bound for the vitality of the ground state. The emphasis (for instance, using angle plunge) could continue to increase the gauge.

In the near future we anticipate there will be a need of new techniques, as both the number of qubits and the number of entry-level tasks increase as we'll never be forced to limit resources. Quantum computers will be able to recreate the properties of energized states and elements like ground state. The majority of classical abdominal muscles code in the form of initio (i.e. that are based on the fundamental laws of nature with no extra assumptions or improbable models) are limited to recreating the static characteristics of grounded state. It is also necessary for new modifications mapping frameworks of molecules that follow either bosonic or fermionic stats onto registers with distinct quantum bits that could be driven by certain equipment networks.

Beyond the material science games themselves There are also opportunities in the related areas of study, such as the display of proteins and elemental elements, climate prediction tranquilize plan, liquid mechanics and computation optics. By utilizing QCs for the classically-unmanageable segments of industrially important problems in sedate structure or different fields, QCs of adequate scale and dependability have the potential for critical business pertinence groupings of activities. According to those who are associated to QEC studies, QEC itself is the crucial task which will run on future QCs. Future research will be required to come up with QEC strategies that are feasible and efficient, which means they will be able to be used more quickly (ie at lower qubit levels) within the technological course of the events.

AI and Optimization

A lot less is known about the use quantum computers in AI but the importance of this application makes it an interesting area of research. If we are able to provide high-dimensional superpositions that contain either the relevant information or some nonlinear capabilities of it, then we will be able to quickly do the tasks of bunching, PCA and other assignments for information analysis. However the state planning that is in place is a challenge to overcome. To achieve a useful speed-up requires setting up the condition of 2n measurements with much less than 2n time and, in the ideal case, within poly(n) duration. The moment, we can only achieve this in certain situations36. This would have great value to broaden the scope of scenarios in which this could be possible.

The adiabatic and variational algorithms to streamlining as well as characterization be executed on quantum computers but are far removed from traditional simulators37. While these techniques provide promising focal points for quantum chemistry, and also simulation38, they've not yet proved to have a superiority over the most well-known classical algorithms. Evidence from experiments using them on quantum computers will enhance our understanding of long-term, continuously adaptable techniques.

Quantum Teleportation And Quantum Theory Of Information

Data is physical, and the processing of data is always carried out using physical methods. It is an unreliable sounding explanation but the results are not insignificant. Over the past few years, there has been an explosion of speculation and test-based advancements that are leading to the creation of a significant new discipline, a distinct Quantum Theory of Information. Quantum material science allows the creation of new types of logic entryways that are completely secure cryptosystems (frameworks that combine the exchange and cryptography) and the encapsulation of two bits of information into one physical object and has, as of recently been proposedas an ancestor of "teleportation".

In the past, the concept of teleportation was never given much thought in the scientific community. In the majority of cases, teleportation is the term used by writers of science fiction essays to the process of having an article, or even an the individual break up in one location and a perfect copy pops in another location.

Usually, this process is completed by filtering the content so as to remove all information from it. At the time this information is transferred to the data it has extracted from then this data is sent to the area that accepts it and utilized to create the replica, but not as the original substance of the original, but likely from molecules of the identical kinds that are orchestrated in the exact same way as the initial. Teleportation machines resemble the fax machine in reality, it will cut through 3-dimensional objects as well as reports. It will create an exact but exact copy, and it would crush the first in the process of in filtering it.

In the classical field of material science, a thing can be moved, at a fundamental level, through the process of estimating to fully describe the characteristics of the object. Data could then be transmitted to a different area and the article is rewritten. Additionally, the classical data theory agrees with the common sense that If a message needs to be sent using an object that is put into one of the N distinct states, the largest amount of messages that can be transmitted is N. A single photons have only two distinct polarization states: left given and right gave. So, a single photon cannot send more than two distinct messages, for instance one data item.

In spite of the basic question can it be feasible to offer a complete copy of the original article? The correct answer is not. The physical frameworks are eventually quantum mechanical . Quantum mechanics shows us that it's difficult to fully determine the state of a mysterious quantum framework which makes it hard to employ the conventional estimation method to evaluate the quantum framework from one region and moving on to the next. This is due to Heisenberg's Uncertainty Principle that states that the more closely an object is scrutinized and scrutinized, the more it gets affected by the filtering process and eventually, one reaches an point at which the item's distinct state has been completely disturbed, but lacking enough information for an accurate copy. This is a convincing argument against 18 teleportation If it is impossible to separate enough information from an object to create an perfect duplicate, it can be evident that a perfect duplicate cannot be created.

Charles H Bennet with his group along with Stephen Wiesner have proposed an unique method of transporting quantum states using EPR states (caught states). Quantum teleportation could be described conceptually as as two particles An as well as B. A has an unidentified state, whichps> spoke to be described as:

|ps> = a|0> + b|1>

This is a single quantum bit (qubit)is it is a quantum framework with two levels. Teleportation's purpose is to transfer the state of the particle From A to. This is achieved by using the snared state. Each gang is one qubit from two qubits caught states;

|ps>(|0>A |0>B) + |1>A|1>B)

The state described above could be modified within the Bell base (|000 >+-|11 >)), (01 >+-|10>) for the first two qubits, and also a contingent one-time change in the stateps> for the third one, which is

(|00>+|11>)|ps>+(|00>-|11>)sZ|ps>   + (|01>+|10>)sX |ps> + (|01>-|10>)(- isY|ps>)

In which sX, sY and SZ are Pauli lattices within the |0>1. A calculation is made using A's qubits within the Bell basis. Based on the outcome of these estimates B's special states areps>, Ps>, sXisZ, ps>. ps> A communicates the outcome of its estimate to B, who will be able to recover the initial state > > by applying the appropriate single change I and s isY, or Y depending on the result of An's estimation. You may notice the quantum transmission hasn't been achieved faster than light, since B has to wait until the result of An's estimation to be delivered before he is able to recover this quantum condition.

Thermodynamics Of Quantum Computation

Computers are machines , and like all machines , they depend on thermodynamics-related essentials, based on how thermodynamic laws work. Similar to any physical structure, modern computers that rely on modern technology generate warmth when they are in use. The most important question is: can computers that are computer-based be improved to minimize the production of heat. It's been discovered that it is possible to imagine (consistent with the principles in the field of materials science) of a computer capable of molds, keeping up with and moving around modern signs, and keeping up with and moving around the latest signs with no heat age. In all likelihood, there is one location where warmth has to be supplied. Once data has been eliminated, the stage space that is associated to the framework which stores the data is repelled. The elimination of a single bit of data reduces the an element of the framework which removed the data at any time S=klog2. This reduction in entropy will bring warming towards the earth.

If it were possible to build a computer that doesn't erase any data, this computer would not generate any kind of warmth at all. This is precisely what happens with quantum computers. Quantum Computation is reversible (however not the readout of the result of the calculation). Therefore, it is possible that, at an elementary scale, to perform quantum calculations without generating heat. Naturally, as a general principle, the computer will generate a lot of heat. Heartbeats of electric energy moving through copper wires must be able to overcome resistance. Electrons that diffuse from the source would in the present time slam into stones and then re-enter the channel by releasing electrons into the channel and again generate heat. In any event it is possible that in the ideal situation copper wires might be replaced with superconductors, in the event of a defect, with official gems.

Quantum computers' reversibility is being recognized by the creation of and creating extraordinary doors. In computers with computers, doors like NAND, NOR, AND and XOR are used. All of these entryways are permanent and will produce heat. The measurement of the data is on the right hand side of (a,b) (ab

This isn't the exact amount of data that is that is located on the left. Making use of Toffoli entranceways Charles Bennett has shown that quantum computers are capable of performing any calculations using only reversible advances. These doors are able to store the information that is transmitted through them with the aim that the computation could be executed forward and in reverse.

This means that the calculation can bring an abundance of information since every intermediate is remembered, however the heat is eliminated that allows the calculation to continue. Once the calculation has been completed, the computation can be performed in reverse, to establish the condition of the computer , and be safe from rapid fire.

Test Realization of Quantum Computer

The ease of engineering makes quantum computers faster smaller, less costly and more efficient however its complex complexities have created a number of difficulties with respect to its acknowledgement of tests. In all likelihood, numerous efforts have been undertaken to get on this goal with a 200% accomplishment. It is anticipated that it won't be long before the quantum computer could replace advanced computers with all its potential. Some of the efforts to test the acceptance of quantum computers are reduced in the following manner:

Heteropolymers:

The first quantum computer was designed and implemented from 1988 Teich and then it was improved through Lloyd during 1993. In a heteropolymer machine, an exact representation of particles serves to serve as memories cells. Data is stored on cells by siphoning the particle in question to an energized state. Instructions are sent to the heteropolymer via laser pulses with precisely tuned frequency. The concept behind the calculation on selected iotas is governed by the form and length that the beat takes.

Ion Traps:

A quantum computer with a particle trap was first thought of by Cirac and Zoller in the year 1995 and was first implemented by Monroe and his colleagues in 1995. It was followed by Schwarzchild in. The computer that is a particle trap encodes information under vitality conditions of particles as well as in vibrational interactions between particles. Theoretically, every particle is scanned by an individual laser. A fundamental analysis showed that Fourier changes can be measured using an instrument called the particle trap. This leads to Shor's thinking calculation that is based upon Fourier changes.

Quantum Electrodynamics Cavity:

The quantum electrodynamics (QED) cavity computer was demonstrated by Turchette and his colleagues in 1995. The computer is made up of an QED pit that's filled with cesium particles, and the course of action of lasers as well as stage move identifiers. mirrors, and polarizers. This is a true quantum computer because it is able to create, manage and control secure the superposition of traps and other superpositions.

Nuclear Magnetic Resonance:

The Nuclear Magnetic Resonance (NMR) computer is comprised of a case filled with a liquid and an NMR machine. Each atom of the fluid acts as a quantum memory record. Calculation continues with heartbeats via radio to the test and analyzing its reactions. Qubits are reconstructed as conditions in the particle cores that comprise the particles. In an NMR computer, the reading out of the memory register is achieved by a calculation based by a statistical instrument made of 2.7×10^{19} particle. This is different from QED pit computer that uses particle trap computers where a single quantum framework was used to read out the memory register.

NMR computers can tackle NP (Non-polynomial) total problems in polynomial-time. The majority of quantum-related achievements in computing have been achieved using NMR computers.

Quantum Dots

Quantum computers that are based upon quantum speck technologies use simpler engineering techniques and less complex testing, theoretical and numerical capabilities when compared with the quantum computer's four uses previously discussed. There are a variety of quantum specks where the dabs are connected to their nearest neighbors through the use of gates for burrowing boundaries, are used to create quantum entrances using the split door techniques. This conspiracy is one of the main central points: qubits are controlled by electrical. The drawback of this technology can be that the quantum bits could communicate with their closest neighbors and sharing information that is that is read out can be very problematic.

Josephson Junctions

The Josephson intersection quantum computer was presented during 1999 by Nakamura as well as his collaborators. In this computer , a Cooper pair box that is a tiny superconducting island , is connected to a mass superconductor. The superconductors' feeble coupling result in an Josephson intersection, which is capacitor. If Cooper box is small enough, Cooper box is not as large in quantum specks, the charging current splits into discrete movements of the individual Cooper sets, and it's now possible to move only a single Cooper pair across the intersection. Similar to quantum dab computers found are used in Josephson computer intersections, called qubits are controlled electronically. Josephson intersection's quantum computing is among the most promising possibilities for the future of quantum computing.

The Kane Computer

This computer resembles quantum speck computers, however in many ways, it's much more of an NMR computer. It is made up of an beautiful and dynamic core of p 31, an isotropically pure gem visually inactive Si. The model is placed within a highly appealing field to make the turning of p 31 to be equal or opposite to the field's direction. The p31core's rotation can then be controlled by using a heartbeat radio frequency to a control anode named A-door, located next to the core.

Electron interspersed communication between twists could be controlled through the application of voltage to terminals known as J-entryways. They are located between the 31cores of the p 31.

Topological Quantum Computer

Qubits in this computer are encoded as the form of the anyons. "Anyons" are quasiparticles in 2-dimensional media that obey the laws of parastatistics (neither Fermi Dirac nor Bose Einstein). In any event the way that anyons remain closer to fermions, due to the assumption that a repugnance resembling a fermion is present between the two. The different evolution of anyons is depicted through interlace gathering. The idea behind the quantum computer that is topological is to use the properties of the plait bunch to represent the movements of anyons in order to carry out quantum calculations. It is believed that a quantum computer should to be able to withstand quantum errors in the topological force of anyons.

Humans and Our Brain

Humans are the dominant species on Earth at the moment. With our population growing to 7 billion, we've conquered nearly every region of the globe. What is it that made us to be among the best-performing species on the planet? Only one definitive answer that is our brain.

The Development of Humans

The human race evolved through an evolutionary process that began with an ancestor who lived for more than 3 million years back. As time passed this ancestor learned to stand on 2 legs , which allowed its forelimbs to control its surroundings. As our ancestors grew they were taught to utilize tools for hunting animals to eat. Once they had controlled fire and learned how to make food from scratch, the growth of our ancestors' early generations exploded.

It's not the truth that humans descend from monkeys. This is a lie. The fact is that modern-day humans as well as monkeys and apes had an ancestor who shared a common ancestor, and consequently evolved in tandem with each other. The situation is similar to a tree, which has one trunk, but many branches. After many evolutionary leaps and many evolutionary steps, we are now the human beings we are currently. However, we didn't begin in this way. There have been many amazing developments in the field of technology and society. These innovations are truly revolutionary and changed the way people lived. The history of the world is filled with these achievements and discoveries that are still in use today but in a more improved and better manner or in a different form. We owe much to the greatest historical figures and women who worked hard , not only to make their lives better, but also the lives of the people around them too.

One of the times when technology really exploded was the twentieth century. There were some amazing and incredible inventions and innovations in this period. Humans were first able to experience flights that were heavier than air in the first half during the 20th century. In the same century that we were able to harness the potential of the atom. Nearly all social sectors benefited from these advances and the society increased in size than it did before.

What was the driving force behind these ideas and inventions? What is the tool these amazing people are using to help their ideas and plans become reality? It's their brains.

The Human Brain

The brain of the human is among the most important organs within our body. It regulates every function in the body. Without it, you'd become a waste of body fluids and cells. The brain has never stopped working every time that it "turned on". It is active when we are active and living the day to day activities as well as when we are asleep in the night.

Evolution

Human brains are the primary driver behind the growth and development of humans. The brain's development is the main reason for why we progressed in to the point we have. What was the process of growth? What are the circumstances that led to the brain growing and evolve into the form it is today?

Human brains were not the same as it is today. It was very similar to neurons of the other primates. Butover the centuries that passed, something occurred that altered the way the human brain is viewed and performs. The most significant variations is dimensions of frontal cortex in the brain. This part of the brain is where the majority of thinking of humans is created. It is the place where the brain's intelligence begins. As time passed the size of our brain increased till it reached the current size. It's not the end of the growth however. The brain might be huge and the human mind can carry out thinking or form ideas, but there are some distinctions among the brains the early human to the modern brain.

The most notable distinct differences is the development of an area within our brains that's exclusively focused on speech. The area is tiny or absent entirely from those of primates however, since humans were taught to speak, this part within the brain grown. The second part of the brain that is different from the brains of our ancestral ancestors is a region known as the Neocortex. The neocortex area is the most modern part of the brain that has was created. This is an brain region that is present only in mammals. The brain's neocortex is responsible for functions of the higher brain such in the control of the perception, intelligence and language. Researchers have discovered that the neocortex develops or at the least development and folds increase in the context of social structures of an individual increases or expands. Therefore, the more social a person is, the more developed their Neocortex might develop.

How does it work

Human brains are among the areas in the body of a human being that has some mysteries to the present. There are some things that are vital to human beings which scientists have not yet been able to identify an area in the brain that controls it. One of those things that are still unsolved or at best, undiscovered is where our consciousness originates. Scientists have been able to map the entire brain, however the root of consciousness yet to be discovered. However, we're not here to discuss what causes consciousness, we're here to gather more knowledge about the way that the brain functions. Let's get started with the process.

The brain operates by with electrochemical signals, which are transmitted to brain cells, also known as neurons that are connected to nearby neurons. These electrical impulses are tiny and traverse the brain, and to the part of the body it regulates. This is the method by which information or messages from the brain are transferred to other areas that make up the human body.

This is also the exact method that the surroundings interact with brain. The sensory organs, similar to the eyes, transmit messages to brain about what they observe and the brain processes those signals to create an image that is coherent. Consider this Imagine a person in a spaceship completely enclosed. The spaceship is travelling through space. Since there are no windows. The individual inside can't be able to directly feel, hear or smell what's happening out there. The ship does have sensors that relay the signals they gather about the exterior of the ship back to the individual. The brain works in exactly the same way. It functions like the individual on the ship. The brain doesn't physically behold, feel or feel the outside world, however, it utilizes the sensory organs in order to send information back to the brain.

Another role that the brain has is control the body. There are numerous activities that occur in the human body even the most basic of things like being able to walk is controlled through the brain. We are accustomed to walking often and it's an automatic process that the human body performs. We do not think much about the manner in which we walk. We usually get the thought of moving in a certain direction and go with it. We don't know the way that the brain regulates it.

However, before we get deeper into the way that the brain functions take a look at the various parts of the human brain.

Major Parts of the Human Brain

Cerebrum

The cerebrum is the largest component of our brain. It is responsible for the majority of the voluntary functions associated with it. The brain is the one that controls the ability to read, feel emotions, learn speech, as well as the movements we think about. When you hear someone say "brain," this is typically the first thing that appears in their mind. The cerebrum has a lot of wrinkles and folds, and that is the main characteristic. The cerebrum is comprised of white and grey matter.

The cerebrum consists of two hemispheres and each hemisphere contains four lobes or sections. The lobes are referred to as temporal, frontal, parietal and the occipital. The frontal lobe is primarily responsible for decision-making and reasoning. The parietal region is responsible for the voluntary movement. The temporal lobe is responsible for speech and sounds and is also responsible for memory. In addition, the occipital region is the one which is responsible for vision.

Cerebellum

The Cerebellum is also known as "Little Brain", is the brain's part located below the cerebrum. It's an inferior version of the cerebrum. Scientists have discovered that this region that is located in the brain "older" than the cerebrum. How is it "older"? Scientists have observed similar structures on primitive reptiles and animals. This indicates that the cerebellum, according to the standard of evolution more ancient than the cerebrum, since even less developed animals have it.

The cerebellum is involved in the coordination of movements. Any injury to it can result in reduction in fine motor control, which results in greater erratic or non-refined movement. The cerebellum plays an important role in learning as well as other functions controlled by the cerebrum but in a less primitive level. The cerebellum and cerebrum regulate the movements and voluntary actions that the body's muscles perform.

Brain Stem

The Brain Stem is located directly below the central part of the cerebrum. It is also located just in the cerebellum's front. This portion of the brain is responsible for the involuntary or automated processes of human brain. These functions are generally essential ones, such as breath and keeping your heart pumping. It also plays a role in the cycles humans undergo, such as sleep cycles and the feeling of hunger. It also regulates the feeling of pain. The brain stem is the main pathway for all signals that come from the cerebrum and entering it. Damage in the brain stem can be deadly and extremely serious.

How the Brain Functions

After we've covered the most important parts in the human brain we can now dive deeper into the inner workings of the brain. As we have said, signals that go to and from the brain pass through neurons. These neurons relay signals on to the next until it gets to either the brain, or an organ that it is connected to. Now, let's examine the way in which a movement can be performed. Let's choose a simple movement such as lifting pen.

The first thing to occurs is when the cerebrum lights up and decides it is ready to take out the pen. What it will do is scan the memory of what a pen's appearance like. It might not be evident, but the part of the brain that makes the decisions the brain isn't the same brain that stores memories, and so the two components communicate with one another. When the correct information about the object is received the signal is transmitted to the eyes to seek out the object. The eye sends an alert that the object is located. The brain transmits a signal to the arm via the brain stem to expand those muscles in the arms fingers and hand to grasp the pen. The nerves in the fingers report that the pen has been placed inside the hand and transmit the signal.

Do you realize the way a simple procedure that we barely notice involves a great many steps? The process of completing this step-by step seems to take a considerable amount of time, however when you actually do it, this entire process is only just a few seconds. The brain performs this process in a way that keeps all other organs of the body functioning.

As you observe, the human brain is an extremely complex machine. It is responsible for a variety of tasks and functions that are crucial to the human condition. In a sense the brain is at the center of all technological and scientific advancements we've made. It is the source of our identity and who we are. It also contains the methods by that we can create the best and brighter future.

Artificial Intelligence

Technology has been an integral part of human development from the beginning. Since the earliest people used sticks and rocks to use as tools to hunt The technology we use developed has been steadily improving. Things we consider to be normal are awe-inspiring to anyone of the past if it were introduced to us. Imagine people as brilliant and shrewd Albert Einstein, arguably one of the most brilliant minds to ever exist stuck and incapable of using computers or smartphones. Imagine someone from a previous time , such as Sir Isaac Newton, being spooked by an airplane or vehicle.

Artificial Intelligence defined

Humans have always longed to improve their lives and, in turn the lives of others surrounding them. This is the source of a number of inventions and discoveries that have transformed the world.

If humans wanted a quicker means of transport that did not require their feet, they hunted animals to ride on. A majority chose horses, while others, particularly within the Middle East, chose camels as well as other kinds of animals. There have been improvements made to enhance this method of transportation. Animals were taught to pull something they could ride on. However, this didn't stop the growth. There were other, more efficient methods of transportation were developed, such as cars and trains. Today there are constant improvements getting made on the technology that human beings already have.

One of the latest inventions that continuously improves has been the computers. Computers revolutionized the way people lived. Since the day it was developed, it changed the way people live. Nowadays, computers that are many hundreds of times faster than first models are now in almost every person's pocket. The computer's operating system has changed as well.

A program is an instruction set which tell computers what it is able to and cannot perform. It also dictates how a computer performs an operation. This could be as simple as showing a word on the screen or one that operates entirely within the background. As time passes and the software has become increasingly complicated. They were initially based on holes on cards that represent the zeros and ones that computers understand. There are now many programming languages that can be utilized to program computers.

The program humans have been playing with is known as Artificial Intelligence. This program's aim is to allow computers to "think" as the human brain. They are able to perform the same things that a human would perform if they were in the same position. That's at least the aim. Complete Artificial Intelligence, or AI machine hasn't been created--at least not yet.

The advancements in computer technology has made AI's that we already have more effective and effective. AI is used in many areas of our lives, including transport, medicine communications, and more. As computers and the programs become more advanced and sophisticated, so will the use of AI. There will be a day that AI controls our daily lives. When that day will occur or if it's advantageous for us is a matter that has no clear answer. However, one thing is certain, AI is in the making and is expected to advance.

Types of AI

There are many instances of AI within our daily lives. In the future, we'll explore the various applications of AI however, for now, let's take a look at the various forms of AI, regardless of whether they is already in existence or not.

Weak AI

Weak AI is the sole kind of AI program we've ever had. They tend to be AI programs that mostly perform only one task in a way. It is sometimes referred to as Narrow AI due to its limited scope of work that it can accomplish. It addresses a specific problem using pre-defined responses to specific questions. It might have some type of speech recognition, however it's not as accurate and might still miss certain aspects. The narrow AI can also be used for repetitive tasks, which guarantees that the products or items made by it are the same in all ways. This type of AI is the one that is most widely used. It is utilized for industries, business, as well as communication. The weak or narrow AI can also be utilized to teach children.

Strong AI

Artificial General Intelligence, or AGI is the primary objective of the people involved in this project. It is often referred to as Strong AI or Full AI. This kind is a type of Artificial Intelligence is considered to be extremely intelligent. It performs all the capabilities that a human brain performs, particularly in problem solving and reasoning. It is also able to learn from its previous experiences.

Another feature that AI has is its capability to create consciousness. Therefore the person who develops this type of AI only has to input the information that he believes the AI needs and have the ability to execute these tasks while the AI will work out the rest by itself. This is the kind of AI often seen in films and science fiction.

The hunt for AGI is in progress and could produce certain results in the near future. The advancement of AGI could help solve many problems but it also could cause other. The details will be covered in the next chapter. However, what we currently have are tests to test Artificial Intelligence programs to determine their "intelligence". The most commonly used kinds of tests is known as"the Turing Test.

The Turing Test, developed by programmers Alan Turing in the 1950's It is a method to test whether an application has "intelligence". This is the way it operates. Humans and computers are in conversation with one another. They are unable to be seen by each other. The test is a series of questions both to the computer and the human. If the test taker or the evaluator is unable to determine the difference between twocomputers, it is deemed to have passed the test.

This is only one of many kinds of tests to determine the degree to which an AI program is "intelligence". For the time being we don't have this type of AI. The impact of this technology or not is dependent on a number of variables.

Superintelligence

The next level above AGI is referred to as superintelligence. This type of AI exceeds the capabilities of all human beings living on this planet. It improves and learns by itself without the aid of other computers or human beings. This is the highest kind of AI that we think of today. Superintelligence doesn't limit itself to computers, however. Future research and studies suggest the possibility of being biological superintelligence. This implies that the human brain can be integrated or enhanced by AGI and enhances his cognitive capabilities.

The AI of the future is still in the process of being discussed whether it's feasible or not. And, in the event that it is what will it mean for the lives of human beings all over the world.

The Uses of AI

Artificial Intelligence, or at most a weak AI is being utilized in every country. Here are a few examples of the present applications of AI in various facets of our society.

Medical

Artificial Intelligence programs are currently being utilized in medical practice to aid doctors to diagnose their patients. AI aids in the creation of "electronic health records" of patients. Robots equipped with AI programmes are utilized in operations. AI can also aid in the development and creation of treatment and drugs for a variety of ailments and ailments.

Transportation

Transportation is among the areas that has been significantly improved by AI programs. From the manufacturing of automobiles to the manner in which the car is operated are assisted or improved by AI. The production of cars as well as the components that make it up are assisted with the help of AI robots.

The most apparent use of AI in transport is the creation autonomous vehicles. These vehicles can safely transport passengers as well as cargo without the assistance of an individual. They look at the road and the surrounding area for the best route to take to transport their cargo. Congestion and traffic could also be reduced through the widespread utilization automated vehicles which can communicate with each other. It's also a method to reduce the risk of road-related accidents.

Business and Economics

AI is also extensively used in the world of business. It is used in many investments and business related decisions. It also helps assist in answering the questions of customers by using "chatbots". Artificial Intelligence technology also utilize algorithms to decide when and where to put advertisements. This increases the profits of a particular business by targeting specific people to the advertisement. AI is also utilized to assist individuals as well as investors with their financial needs. It makes use of the data to develop algorithms that determine the best way to invest money to make the most profits.

Video games

Many video games employ the term AI to describe the game. However, there is a type of AI that is modeled after the human way of playing the game. This is most commonly applied in FPS (First-Person-Shooting) and MMORPG (Massively Multiplayer Online Role

Playing Game) games. Programmers have created an AI program which learns from the playing way of humans and then mimics or improves on the style of play. AI programs are also employed for "cheat" on some games.

Military

These vehicles are in use within the militaries for quite a time. There are many planes, including Predator Drone, for instance. Predator Drone, that does not have a real pilot sitting in the cockpit. Instead the plane is controlled remotely by a pilot in an uninvolved area. AI is used in military to eliminate the human element of the process completely. The development of autonomous ships tanks, and submarines are being carried out by many of the most technologically advanced countries. Another possibility for using AI to combat in military operations is the creation of an artificial soldiers or the combatant. Instead of humans on the battlefield, risking their lives, robots as well as autonomous vehicles could be employed to reduce casualties.

Construction & Manufacturing

The process of designing and planning buildings requires lots of calculations to make sure the safety and security of the structure. AI is used to make quick plans and calculations that help architects and engineers more efficient. Autonomous construction equipment and vehicles are being created. This is not just efficient for the work , but also enhances the security of the construction site.

When it comes to manufacturing and the production of products, AI is being widely employed. It is mostly used to create robots. They accomplish tasks that are not possible or dangerous to humans. Robotic arms can also perform tedious and complex tasks during the production of the product. This helps reduce errors in production and reduces the chance of accidents.

The Future of AI

The rapid advancement and development that is being made by AI programs will certainly have an an impact on the way people live their lives. Like I said this change could be either beneficial or harmful for us, or both. Whichever way you look at it Artificial Intelligence is in the process of developing further and it is expected to remain in our lives. Let's look at the how Artificial Intelligence is going to influence human lives in the near future, particularly when AI programs AI software programs have similar "intelligence" as humans.

There are a few issues which need to be answered however. Are the developments of AI and, specifically AGI legal? What will a computer program look at us? Does it be conscious? What can a person do to manage it? There are a few questions that can be answered within this article.

Many people, particularly those who are following the news in science, are excited about the advancement of sophisticated AI. The technology available illustrates the benefits and potential disadvantages in AI systems. While the present data indicates that AI is positive, there are people who are worried about what the advancement of artificial intelligence that is human-like or close to artificial intelligence can result in. What will it do to improve our lives? Many studies show that AI offers a variety of benefits that enhance the way that humans live. However the fear of developing AI is not a matter of throwing it aside. These are issues that the makers of AI will need to resolve before they occur. Giving the world assurance that AI is secure will ensure that it is popular and totally beneficial for humans.

Let's now examine a more optimistic and pessimistic views of AI and the things it is able to accomplish.

The Optimistic View

The growth of AI can bring about future research studies predicting the brighter and better future for humans as well as their lives. Enhancing the everyday routine is among the objectives for AI developers. They are determined to help human beings do things quicker, more secure, and efficient. The AI programs that we have prove this. Autonomous vehicles, robots and financial advisors who are digital are only a few ways that AI is currently making life better for people from all over the world.

However, these are only the benefits that we can enjoy right now. What will the future hold? As we've seen earlier there are lots of applications for AI. However, its value does not stop there. As AI systems become increasingly sophisticated and powerful, they will affect numerous aspects that will be beneficial to our lives in the future. Let's talk about these issues.

One of the most significant things that could be altered when AI becomes more prevalent and sophisticated is the transportation industry. Autonomous vehicles won't only be more common and widely used, but they'll probably become the primary mode of transportation for everybody. Some have compared these autonomous vehicles to the humans' red blood cells. When the cells move through your body they move independently of each other. They arrive at their destination without any problems or accidents, regardless of how small the blood vessels are. This concept is used to design autonomous cars, particularly in the area of security. Around the world, millions of people get injured or killed in accidents on the roads each year. Since the introduction of self-driving vehicles, this number will be drastically reduced since they are cognizant of what's happening around them, and respond to their surroundings much faster than human drivers can. If a single network manages all cars in the roads, these vehicles are able to communicate with each other and adjust their speed, route and direction based on what's happening around them. This not only makes roads more efficient and more efficient, but it can also dramatically improve safety on the roads.

Another advantage that modern AI has to offer is that it is also linked to security. However, this time it's directly connected to human beings. AI, or specifically, robots, don't suffer pain. Additionally, they are able to be fixed if they're damaged or destroyed. This means that they could replace the risky jobs that humans are currently performing. Mining welding, mining, operating heavy equipment as well as working in nuclear reactors are just a few of the more dangerous jobs humans do. As technology advances, AI robotics, the tasks or at the very least, the risky parts of these tasks will be carried out by machines that are more affordable to replace and are less important as human life. However, this doesn't mean that humans will be entirely out of the picture. Humans may be tasked with overseeing the robots when they are performing their duties. Another risky task that robots are capable of performing has to be related to the police force. Robots are able to disperse bombs or eliminate dangers to humans. Robots can also be employed to explore space and the ocean. Due to the

162

harsh environment in these environments humans are unable to go directly to them to explore. Through AI and robots they could be used to investigate or as early settlements to make way for humans to make the planet accessible to them, particularly when they travel to other planets. In addition, AI be employed for risky tasks, but they could also be employed for boring or boring tasks. AI doesn't require breaks or breaks and can perform any small or large job by itself. AI robots can also serve as police officers, soldiers or soldiers. A lot of money cannot ever buy the life of a human being, therefore robots could be employed as a substitute for human beings when fighting the adversaries.

AI or at the very most, a portion of it, may be integrated directly with a person to enhance the capabilities of that person. This is referred to as augmenting. Humans can incorporate things into the body permanently that can improve their brain power as well as their physical endurance. This technology is also employed for prosthetics as well as medicine.

If a specific part of the body requires replacing, an autonomic component could be designed to feel and behaves like the original piece. Nearly everyone has an iPhone nowadays. What if in the future, we don't require phones that are physically accessible? What if the phone was already within you? It's all you have to do is think about calling someone. Then you'll be able speak to them directly without having to do anything physical. This sounds like science fiction does it not? At the moment this is still. However, in the near future, when more advanced and superior AI enters the world it could be the future we live in. The strength of our bodies is also able to be significantly enhanced. By enhancing their strength, we are able to become stronger, faster and smarter than ever before.

One of the major issues humankind is facing right present is the climate change. Alongside the increase in global temperatures there are a number of storms and hurricanes have devastated many nations. There's also been an increase in droughts and other diseases. As technology advances and improves, of AI technology, AI can be utilized to combat and address these issues. AI and other advanced algorithms can aid in predicting the likelihood of natural disasters to happen. This can help increase the speed at which we respond to circumstances, which could ensure the lives of many. Advanced AI could enhance the overall health of everyone. For instance, superintelligence might be able to determine how to distribute the wealth that the planet has, making certain that no one be starving. Famine and war could also be rendered obsolete by AI developments, since many conflict is fought for resources.

AI when used in robots, can create an artificial companion or friend. They also can serve as human servants. This can be extremely helpful to people in need of individual care and care. This means that elderly care and hospitals facilities will not need to hire a large number of individuals to care for their patients. Another benefit is that robots aren't tired and don't need breaks. Robots operate 24 hours a day, 7 days a week. This is ideal for ICU's and hospitals which care for many patients simultaneously. Robots can also be allies for patients who require them, particularly those suffering from mental health problems. Being able to talk to someone who is able to understand and comprehend the issues they're experiencing can significantly aid in their treatment.

The Pessimistic View

Although there are certainly numerous benefits associated with the advancement of AI but there are certain risks. Humans are generally tolerant of the possibility of change. This is the reason we thrive. Humans' ability to adapt to their environment is the reason we are the most dominant species on the planet. However, we haven't yet come across something that could fundamentally alter how we live and thrive in such a drastic way. The majority of changes that happen in the history of mankind are gradual and their effects are only felt perhaps an entire generation after the invention. With the advances in AI and computer technology the speed of developments has increased exponentially, and the consequences of innovations and advancements have been felt by those who are in that same age group. As a result, as we witness the creation and development of ever advanced AI systems what will it mean for human lives? Is it going to be always positive? Do we ever have the world of utopia? While some research studies will demonstrate the advantages of modern AI technology but there are grave risks to be aware of. Let's examine them in greater detail.

AI and robots are able to do lots of tasks in the past, as was stated. They are currently performing basic tasks that are hard or dangerous for humans to perform. But what happens if in the future, AI systems become more advanced, they could accomplish everything humans are able to do and even better? What impact will this have on our lives? It is a real issue that is occurring, but at a lower scale. Are you aware of the robots doing the small, monotonous tasks right now? They were previously performed by people before. Someone with food for his family and children to take to school as well as bills that need to be paid. Since a computer can perform the work more efficiently and quicker than any human could ever it, he's been removed from the workforce. This is a scenario that is occurring all over the world. Workers, particularly those who aren't skilled are being replaced with machines that are able to do their job. This is advantageous to the proprietor of the business which employs them since they will no longer be required to pay the salaries of one person. He'll be responsible for the entire machine and perhaps some upkeep, which is cheaper than hiring a worker. What happens when you change jobs? How will it affect the person who's been fired? The situation is does not just affect the worker but all those who have to rely on him. At present there are only a few small and easy jobs are being replaced however, if all tasks are now being performed by AI, computers and robots? What do we humans have to do? Will we be totally dependent on computers and robots to run our life? However, robots aren't just capable of taking over minor tasks. As they become more sophisticated, they could replace skilled workers , even professionals. This is known as technological unemployment. Technological unemployment is that humans are replaced with machines to perform their tasks. This can lead to unemployment and poverty for people who are not employed. This is one of the scenarios that researchers are concerned about due to the rapid development of AI technology.

Another possible scenario that stems from the more advanced artificial intelligence systems could be the total destruction or subjugation of humanity with these machines. We are all aware that humans are the most technologically advanced species on earth. We have controlled the planet and made use of it to enhance ourselves. We have utilized and continue to making use of the natural resources Nature gives us. We have slowed down the number of species of animals we have encountered even wild ones like tigers and lions. Many have become our pets or even food sources for us. What happens if we become substituted by AI systems that are the most powerful technology on earth? What happens to us? Are we going to be the slaves of computers? Or will they totally eliminate the human race? These are only a few of the concerns which AI developers and scientists are trying to find answers. They are seeking ways to regulate the behavior of an AI program, even the time it gets smarter than the smartest person who ever lived.

One scenario that researchers are worried about isn't that AI is able to develop consciousness and decides to eradicate humanity. What they are worried about is that its objectives might differ from those of the person who invented it. As AI systems grow increasingly intelligent they may come up with their own goals that don't have anything to do with its initial purpose. Another concern is that the objectives for the designer and system could be compatible, but the method by the process of achieving the AI's objective could be destructive. It could be rushing headlong into the pursuit of its goal, without considering the impact of its actions on the world. In these situations, complete control of the AI is essential.

One of the most realistic threats for modern AI systems is that they could be employed for destructive purposes. Even powerful governments and terrorists once they have access to an effective weapon, will seek ways to utilize it against their adversaries. What can keep the terrorists from "weaponizing" an advanced AI program to carry out the dirty work? For instance terrorists could launch a bomb in an area with a lot of people, but without risking the lives of one of their own members. They could simply send an automated vehicle to a certain location. They could even get into the network of their targets and steal sensitive documents from them. Nations and countries could use advanced AI to attack their own citizens to remain in the position of power. This is taking place without the assistance or assistance of AI systems. Imagine how hazardous it would be if AI program is assisting them to accomplish this. It is impossible to stay protected from their presence.

Humans and AI

In an interview on BBC interview in December 14, 2014, the physicist Professor. Stephen Hawking said that "The development of full artificial intelligence could spell the end of the human race ....It would take off on its own, and re-design itself at an ever-increasing rate. Humans, who are limited by slow biological evolution, couldn't compete and would be superseded." This is among the concerns that a majority of people are concerned about. AI technology. It gets improving with each improvement. We'll look at the specifics of what AI technology could create significant changes in our lives. Let's see if these changes are good or bad for us.

Human Workers VS AI Workers

The advent of the automobile has drastically changed life of horse. Horses were once the main mode of transportation for all. They were employed in cities as a method to travel, they were utilized to transport products and cargo across long distances. They were also used in mines and farms, and even to fight. However, the advent of the automobile , things changed. The horses were replaced by automobiles, despite the fact that the first automobiles were slower than horses. The advantages of cars over horses comes from economics. The expense of owning horses and keeping them is much more costly than the upkeep of cars. They also provided more power , but at a lower price. One automobile could be as powerful as five or four horses. The automobiles didn't have to be superior to the horse. It just required to perform the same task as the horse at the same price.

This has been the case in the past, and will likely to occur once more. Similar to how horses have been replaced with cars human beings are also being replaced by robots as well as automated machines for their jobs. This is not limited to jobs in factories and also to professionals. A large number of factories workers have been replaced with automated machines that performed their work the same way they had always done. The machines, or robots were not required to be better or faster than human beings. They might possess similar capabilities. What makes them different that makes them more financially feasible than human beings, is the fact that they never run out of energy. They can last for decades with minimal maintenance. While a human worker requires breaks for food and rest throughout the day. This gave a significant advantage to the machines , which made them replace humans in production lines and factories. Of sure, there are people who work on the machinery, however the quantity of workers in one manufacturing line has decreased from hundreds to only 10 people across the entire line.

Machines, robots, and computer programs get better and more efficient and more efficient, they are likely to take over more and more human beings in increasing numbers of tasks as time goes by. Automated vehicles are advancing and is already guiding this change. Transportation has a large number of employees across the globe, around 70 million according to estimates. The autonomous vehicle could take over these drivers simply because they're more financially feasible. A self-driving vehicle has numerous advantages over the human driver. Human drivers are exhausted, sleepy, or get distracted, and may need to take a break every once every once in a while. A computerized truck doesn't. Even something as simple like a break in the bathroom can affect the efficiency of workers. Therefore, as computers become more advanced every day, increasing numbers of people will be unemployed and not because they're incompetent or don't meet the criteria for employment but because they are not needed any more. In the near future there could be signs that state"Humans Do Not Need to Apply" "Humans Do Not Need to Apply".

However, these jobs aren't the only ones that could be substituted. Professionals can also become ineligible or even no longer required to perform the tasks they perform. There is currently a program known as Watson that can provide medical diagnoses to a majority of patients with precision. Watson provides diagnoses based upon a multitude of variables and factors that human experts are not able to be able to match. Even the jobs lawyers do are doing, or at most their writing can be completed by computers. Because computers don't require rest, sleep or eat and drink water, they're more efficient than humans. This is in addition to the fact that computers can process many thousands of files in just a couple of hours, as opposed to weeks for humans is already making them more efficient. What this means is that history is repeating itself. As more sophisticated computer software and AI software are created, more and more jobs will be eliminated for human beings. However, there is hope but. There is, obviously there is still some doubt about the idea that humans are going to be substituted by computers and robots. There are still tasks, or professions, that computers and robots can't accomplish. The list of jobs is getting smaller by the day. What can we do? take to stop it?

One thing being investigated is ways to limit the surge and surge of computers entering the workplaces of human beings. Companies are still trying to find ways to hire people for various jobs. Programmers are also looking for ways to work in order to prevent people from lose control of AI software and other systems. With the advancement of computer-based programming technology, humans have little control on the creation of AI programs. The concept of machine learning. This means that computers are learning by itself based on the data being fed to it. However, humans are still in charge of the amount and type of data fed to the computer. There are programmers who develop AI systems in which humans' input is necessary. For instance the AI program named AIVA can create music that is enjoyable to the ears , and appears to be created by humans since its creators provided it with the information that it needs for this to be able to function. Thus, in a way even though AI programs get increasingly sophisticated yet, there's humans in the loop. The job of this person could be as easy as turning off a light or pressing a button when they feel that something is wrong. Certain AI doubters are even suggesting that each AI system will require an individual on the other end of the line to transfer data and data into it. This means that some people are not concerned about AI systems taking over their jobs. However, we need to confront the possibility that someday, humans are no longer required to work as an AI program will do the job for them. What will make this beneficial or not is not sure. We do know that it is possible that this is the direction the future is heading.

The Brain VS AI Brains

A AI program is in essence an artificial model that mimics the brain of a human. It is attempting to emulate exactly what our brains are capable of doing. This is exactly what the is currently being done by AI programmers are trying to achieve. They are trying to develop the AI system that functions like humans' brains. We are all aware humans are complex machine. It is also the most complicated machine we have ever seen, yet it is an actual machine. Its functions, the parts and the role of each individual part are being researched right now. There are some aspects that are already understood by the way it functions. The trick is to translate it to input which computers and AI systems can understand. This is a lot more difficult than it appears. As was demonstrated before in this publication the act of getting a pen in the air requires many actions and choices that our brains make nearly instantaneously.

People have been comparing human brain with computers for quite a while. Of sure, there are tasks where AI computer programs can do superior to humans however, humans have a superior brain than AI programs for simpler tasks, and decisions. In the present, AI programs are capable of performing basic tasks, but as time passes by and technology develops, more, they are getting with humans faster. In the past computers were huge machines that were as big as an entire room. Today, you can find computers that fit in everyone's pockets. This is the pattern that technology seems to be following. Technology is being applied to create better and more efficient technology. Thus, a general purpose AI may not be feasible in the near future, but it is possible that they will be available in the near future. Who is to say?

Let's look at the contrast between the artificial brain and a human artificial intelligence which aims to duplicate it. There are several aspects that humans as well as AI programs could be compared against each other. They include energy efficiency the processing capacity, its universal usage as well as multi-tasking. We'll now look at further details about these aspects.

Energy Efficiency

Our brain is strong machine. This is as we've discovered earlier. The thing that most people aren't aware of is how efficient the energy usage is. The human brain uses about 25 watts to function, whereas devices that are just near to replicating the human brain consume about 2000 watts. The human brain is considerably smaller and more efficient even though it takes more power than the digital version. This is among the areas where the human brain has a huge advantage over the AI systems. It is important to keep in mind that the AI systems we currently have and even the most advanced ones, aren't even close to being able to replicate humans' brain.

Therefore, a general-purpose AI that works in exactly the same way the human brain might require a greater amount of energy than the systems exist today.

Processing Power

The most significant benefit that comes with AI computers over humans is the capacity and the amount of data the computer is able to process. We are all aware that computers can beat the human brain in terms processing capability. A AI system is able to process millions of information simultaneously and process them faster and more precisely than a human brain can. This is among the major reasons AI applications are currently being created. The amount of information is available to us has increased every day since the invention of computers. The Internet has also changed the way data was transferred. Another factor that provides AI systems an advantage against human minds is the fact that they are not tired. AI systems don't get exhausted and are able to function 24/7 seven days of the week. In contrast to humans who need to rest for a few hours to be able to function properly and perform their tasks but an AI system doesn't. It is also a lot more precise than humans. Because it is processing a huge amount of information at the same at the same time, it is able to make deductions and correlations based upon the information it's got. This cuts down the chance of error to a zero. The precision of these systems is superior to human beings in categorizing and sorting things. As icing on the cake the AI system could be utilized to take the place of a human for routine tasks that are boring and monotonous, like reviewing inventories and paperwork.

Universal Use

As we've already proven that the human brain is still as the standard by the level of which AI systems are compared to. The human brain is universal in its tasks. It can perform everything it is required to do, without relying on any other machine or brain to accomplish it. If there's something humans do not understand however, it will be capable of learning about it, in a relatively short time. AI systems, however are currently capable of performing only one thing at an time. Even the most sophisticated AI systems aren't even close to what the brain of a human. Learning for humans can take several hours or days to master a new skill. In contrast, AI systems need a couple of weeks or even months before they are able to accomplish even a single task. The reason? The human brain might be well-known however, it's difficult to create inputs for the specific task that a computer or AI system can comprehend. This is the main limitation that AI systems as well as any other computer program are faced with. Human brains are necessary for an artificial brain work. The data and input required by an AI system requires are being fed to it by humans. It is true that it can learn from previous calculations, but this takes a lot of time to complete.